# THE INDIGI
# TO PARLIAMENT?

## *DON'T RISK IT*

# THE NO CASE

PETER O'BRIEN

Connor Court Publishing

CONNOR COURT PUBLISHING PTY LTD
PO Box 7257
Redland Bay QLD 4165
sales@connorcourt.com
www.connorcourt.com

ISBN: 9781922815477


Cover design by Maria Giordano



Printed in Australia

*A nation for a continent and a continent for a nation*
Edmund Barton
First Prime Minister of Australia

# FOREWORD

Peter O'Brien, soldier and strong defender of constitutional government and of the rule of law, is an ideal person to present the No case in the referendum for an indigenous Voice to Parliament and to the government.

There are already some similarities with the last federal referendum, the 1999 republic referendum. As national convenor of Australians for Constitutional Monarchy I have a unique perspective, ACM being the only extant organisation with living experience of delivering a successful No Case.

There are already similarities.

The No Case today is impoverished, the Yes flush with funds. The No case, I suspect, is stronger in the outer suburbs and the regions while the Yes case will prevail in the elite inner city electorates.

Early polling indicated overwhelming success for the Yes case, but this is receding. The Yes case has not even approached the bar suggested by the founders who inserted the constitutional safeguard of a double majority.

As founders Sir John Quick and Sir Robert Garran observed, this safeguard was not to prevent or resist change but rather, to prevent change being made by haste or by stealth.

It was to encourage public discussion and to delay change until there is strong evidence that it is 'desirable, irresistible and inevitable'.

This bar was never reached in 1999, despite the media and it seems unlikely in this referendum.

Given that Australians are a wise constitutional people, I suspect that this referendum is already doomed.

My observation about the wisdom of the Australian people will not be shared by the elites, who are constantly outraged that Australians have only approved eight out of forty-four federal referendums.

Remembering that the Constitution – in my view unwisely – restricts the power to call referendums to the Canberra politicians, it is not surprising that the ones rejected were either to give them more power or to remove or loosen a sensible restriction on them.

If you look at the ones rejected, most of those about power would be superfluous today.

Too many have been given to the Canberra politicians, to a greater or lesser degree by the High Court, a good reason not to trust that body to interpret the Voice.

This is particularly so when it is recalled that on matters indigenous, the High Court has a record of going to water.

Now there is one thing that distinguishes the republic referendum from the Voice referendum.

As I wrote in Spectator Australia, the conduct of the Voice referendum is the sleaziest yet known.

The Labor leaders in the Fisher government who early last century set up the Yes/No booklet to ensure the people were properly informed of the official cases for and against a referendum, would be appalled.

John Howard set the gold standard for the proper conduct of a modern referendum in 1999, although when the Turnbull republicans lost, they blamed him by concocting stories about his alleged misbehaviour.

They hoped the mainstream media would forget the ovation the Turnbull republicans gave Howard when he allowed them to put their preferred model to the people, notwithstanding that it failed to gain the required absolute majority at the Constitutional Convention.

Albanese's conduct of the referendum is, frankly, worthy of a banana republic. The strategy has been to gag the No case and ensure it has no funds. The Bill to change the conduct of the referendum, the Referendum (Machinery Provisions) Amendment Bill, is an outrage, as I explained in a detailed and accessible submission to the Joint Standing Committee on Electoral Matters.

One tactic of some Yes case proponents is truly below the belt. This is to portray opponents as racist.

I, for one, am no racist. How could I be? When, over a century ago, my grandparents came from what is now Indonesia to buy a farm here, to comply with the White Australia Policy they were given an English dictation test which even their infants, including my mother, passed with flying colours. They were allowed to stay by, I suspect, a kindly customs officer.

Following the principle 'never whinge and never cringe', none of us ever did, even while lapping up the nation's leading magazine published under the banner 'Australia for the White Man'.

When I was a young man, I couldn't do those wonderful things politicians, executives, and other elites now regularly do for the indigenous cause – attending 'Welcome to Country' ceremonies, flying an indigenous flag which did not exist then, lending credence to what some say is the fabrication of Aboriginal history and throwing other peoples' money, taxpayers' and shareholders', into the Yes case for this Voice.

Rather than all this, I could only volunteer to work with the then non-profit non-government Aboriginal Legal Service founded by a future judge, Hal Wootten.

Years later, when I was to move the vote of thanks to Prime Minister Tony Abbott for delivering Australians for Constitutional Monarchy's (ACM) Neville Bonner Oration, I was surprised when he called on us, as the 'fiercest defenders of the constitution', to support indigenous constitutional recognition.

I suggested that the Australian people be involved, not just in the vote at the end, but from the very beginning.

This, I said, could be done by holding a long-overdue people's convention reviewing, for the first time, our more than one-century-old constitution.

So, ACM made a submission along these lines to the 2015 Parliamentary Committee on Indigenous Recognition. The main comment at the hearing, I recall, was one MP's outrage at our proposal that delegates not be paid.

At that time the prevailing view was that indigenous recognition could be achieved by several confusing and to an extent contradictory changes to the constitution. It was obvious they would never have been passed in a referendum.

When reality prevailed and they were dropped, to our surprise, ACM's idea of a convention took off. But not one representing all Australians. Just an indigenous one at Uluru. That was not just for a voice but for a treaty and truth-telling and a separate state , as Keith Windschuttle argues in the book The Break-up of Australia.

In this pamphlet Peter O'Brien sets out the many reasons to cast a No vote in this referendum. They should be known and discussed across the country. There is an onus on the Yes case to answer each.

To the undecided, the advice of the nation's leading broadcaster

Alan Jones in 1999 remains relevant, especially as the government seems intent on hiding much about the referendum: 'If you don't know, Vote No.'

David Flint

Emeritus Professor of Law

# INTRODUCTION

Sometime in the near future, Australians will be asked to vote to establish a consultative body, known as the Indigenous Voice to Parliament and the Government, in our Constitution. Judging by the polls, this initiative has wide support, with many people seeing it as a) only fair that Aboriginal people should be consulted on the framing of legislation that might affect them and b) long overdue recognition of the presence of Aboriginal people on this continent for thousands of years before they were dispossessed by British colonization.

The aim of this booklet is to present a comprehensive case against the Voice by covering all the various issues, many of which have been singly highlighted in articles and speeches by prominent Australians, such as Senator Jacinta Price and Warren Mundine. This booklet will tell you all you need to know to make a fully informed decision.

The proposal comingles two issues – advice to Parliament and constitutional recognition – which is problematic in itself. Any change to the Constitution should be simple, focussed and designed to address one particular problem. This Voice is a chameleon. I will develop this theme further throughout this booklet. And I will argue that the Voice will not be content to remain an advisory body and will, sooner rather than later, seek to exert power in its own right.

But what many people do not realize is that, if successful, this would be a major change to the Constitution – by far the most radical it has ever undergone – and it would fundamentally change the Constitution into a document it was never intended to be.

The claim is made that the Constitution is flawed or incomplete because it fails to mention the Aboriginal people. I will show that this notion is false.

And, a fundamental point which needs to be made right up front is that the Constitution, by virtue of Section 51(xxvi), already gives Parliament the power to establish this Voice under legislation. From the perspective of providing advice, it does not need to be in the Constitution.

Much of the debate in support of the Voice is based on emotion and rhetoric rather than facts. This is intended to foster a sense of guilt in white Australians so that they will more readily accede to what is being proposed. Much of this guilt is based on false beliefs. I will address many of these beliefs later, even though they might appear peripheral to the central question of the Voice. My contention is that the Voice needs to be considered within the whole context of Aboriginal grievance. In particular, to what extent is it a practical imperative and to what extent is it an ideological one.

In mid 2022 Prime Minister Anthony Albanese announced he will hold a referendum, probably late in 2023. The draft form of the proposed amendment is:

- There shall be a body, to be called the Aboriginal and Torres Strait Islander Voice.

- The Aboriginal and Torres Strait Islander Voice may make representations to Parliament and the Executive Government on matters relating to Aboriginal and Torres Strait Islander Peoples.

- The Parliament shall, subject to this Constitution, have power to make laws with respect to the composition, functions, powers and procedures of the Aboriginal and Torres Strait Islander Voice.

This has prompted much debate about the lack of details of the Voice itself, although I think this argument can be over-stated. Certainly, we don't know exactly what will be proposed, but we have a pretty good idea, based on extensive work already done by the Voice Co-Design Committee headed by Professors Marcia Langton and Tom Calma.

It is the exact wording of the referendum question that is critical at this point. Not the fine details of the Voice that might ultimately be legislated if the referendum succeeds.

Ideally, a provision in the Constitution should not be over-prescriptive – it should offer room for reasonable interpretation in the face of evolving social and political imperatives. But neither should it provide *carte blanche* to the Parliament. Such a provision relating to the Voice should, as a bare minimum, specify its basic functions, how its members are to be selected and constraints on its powers. It would then be up to Parliament to prescribe the procedures – certainly not the functions and powers – under which it will operate i.e., to come up with a working model.

The wording above falls a long way short of this. For example, a provision in the Constitution that references, or rather preferences, a certain group of people, must make it beyond doubt who those people are. If the current criterion – self-identification – is applied, that would open up a can of worms. We need to know who exactly qualifies as an Aborigine and how those persons establish their *bona fides*. For example, would any degree of Aboriginality in one's ancestry qualify? If so, then the Aboriginal population can only continue to expand indefinitely, to the point where this will become less and less about disadvantage and more and more about entitlement. If not, then where is the cut-off? 50% aboriginality? 25%? 12.5%? Wherever it is set, someone is going to be aggrieved. To further complicate the issue, prominent Aboriginal academic, Dr Suzanne Ingram, suggests that as many as 300,000 of the currently reported Aboriginal population of 800,000 may not be genuine. If this issue is not adequately addressed in the referendum question itself, that alone should be a deal breaker. I cannot stress this enough. It cannot be left up to Parliament, or worse the High Court, to define, expand or contract this demographic at whim. If the Voice goes into the Constitution, then it must be the Constitution (by means of a referendum) that defines and redefines – over time and as necessary – who is an Aborigine.

We often hear the refrain 'If the government can make laws for Aboriginal people, then we should have a say in the framing of those laws. That's only fair'. That is one of the more simplistic justifications for the Voice, nonetheless its very simplicity gives it some force. It is based on a false premise, as I shall show. Nonetheless it is a proposition that will appeal to many people. However, the proposed referendum question above does not accurately reflect this sentiment. All laws affect Aboriginal people. Are they then to have an extra say in laws that affect the general population? That is what the above wording suggests. That would be patently unfair. The wording above should be amended to say that the Voice may make representations 'only on laws relating exclusively to Aboriginal and Torres Strait Islanders, i.e., those enacted under Section 51(xxvi) of the Constitution'.

Another fundamental requirement would be the inclusion of a specific caveat that its advice is not binding on Government, since that is the claim of all Voice proponents. In fact, I will later argue that even this caveat would not be watertight, but it should be there as a starting point.

As it stands, and despite the wording of clause 2 – the Voice 'may make representations' – clause 3 suggests that Parliament could give it any powers it wishes. That is certainly *carte blanche*.

I imagine that the shortcomings I have outlined above, and others, might be addressed as the process advances, but regardless of that, the real problem is that this whole proposal is fundamentally flawed.

On 23 March 2023, just as this book was going into print, Prime Minister Anthony Albanese released the final referendum question that will be put to the people sometime between October and December 2023. The proposed question is:

> A Proposed Law: to alter the Constitution to recognise the First Peoples of Australia by establishing an Aboriginal and Torres Strait Islander Voice.
>
> Do you approve this proposed alteration?

The proposed amendments to the Constitution are:

> Chapter IX Recognition of Aboriginal and Torres Strait Islander Peoples
>
> 129 Aboriginal and Torres Strait Islander Voice
>
> In recognition of Aboriginal and Torres Strait Islander peoples as the First Peoples of Australia:
>
> > There shall be a body, to be called the Aboriginal and Torres Strait Islander Voice;
> >
> > The Aboriginal and Torres Strait Islander Voice may make representations to the Parliament and the Executive Government of the Commonwealth on matters relating to Aboriginal and Torres Strait Islander peoples;
> >
> > The Parliament shall, subject to this Constitution, have

> power to make laws with respect to matters relating to the Aboriginal and Torres Strait Islander Voice, including its composition, functions, powers and procedures.

This wording addresses none of the problems I have outlined above. And, indeed, it has attracted severe criticism from one of the staunch proponents of the concept of a Voice, constitutional law Professor Greg Craven. He recommended that advice to the executive government should be dropped as he believes it has the potential to severely impact the smooth operation of government – in all areas not just those relating uniquely to Aborigines – through legal challenges. I address this issue in later chapters.

The Referendum Working Group was strongly advised by the Attorney-General and the Solicitor-General to amend the wording to take account of the concerns of Professor Craven and others in order to assuage community concerns and strengthen the case for the Voice, but it rejected this advice out of hand. Even though it is yet to emerge from the womb, the Voice has effectively exercised its first veto. This does not bode well for the supremacy of Parliament.

In this booklet I will present a case against the Voice proposal based on the Co-Design Report. I will argue that even a legislated Voice will be disruptive and divisive at worst, and an expensive white elephant at best.

And I will argue that, even if the Voice *were* effective, it would have no place in our Constitution. Being in the Constitution will not guarantee its effectiveness. Proponents argue that putting the Voice in the Constitution provides a practical, rather merely symbolic, means of achieving Constitutional recognition. That presupposes that Constitutional recognition is a desirable thing. I will argue later that this is not so. And I will also argue that, in any case, the Constitution is not an appropriate vehicle for symbolism – which is subjective and open to misinterpretation or reinterpretation. But how ironic it would be if Aborigines achieved their goal of Constitutional recognition by means of a flawed institution.

The other reason advanced for constitutional 'enshrinement', i.e., to prevent it being abolished, is the very reason why it should *not* be in the Constitution.

I will examine the Uluru Statement of the Heart which forms the basis of the proposal, and I will explain the history and nature of the Constitution, such that readers will be able to form their own conclusion as to whether or not the two concepts are compatible.

And I will show that the Constitution has not failed Aboriginal people, which is perhaps the most important point, since much of the rhetoric surrounding this dangerous proposal is based on that claim.

I will argue that this referendum, if it is successful, will be divisive. But even by virtue of the fact that it is being put, it is also divisive. Referenda are notoriously difficult to achieve in Australia. In 120 years, only 8 of 44 referenda have succeeded. The last significant proposed change – the so-called Australian Republic – bolstered by apparent widespread support, failed spectacularly. It's supporters, although disappointed, accepted the result and quietly got on with working towards a new attempt, as is their right.

There is every chance this Voice referendum will also fail. But this failure will not be accepted with quiet resignation and a determination to simply legislate the Voice as a consolation prize. Aboriginal leader, Noel Pearson, makes it clear that this is not about advice. He has said:

> The voice is and was all about constitutional recognition. Whatever was done in the wake of the failure of the voice at a referendum, it wouldn't be the voice. We'd just probably wind back the clock and go 'the government of the day can decide to establish a completely useless indigenous advisory body'.

Why would the Voice be effective if it were in the Constitution, but the same body be 'completely useless' if it were simply legislated? This tells you that there is another agenda at work here.

Failure of the referendum will be attended by shrieks of racism, protests and possibly violence. That would be a regrettable situation, but preventing such an outcome would be a very flimsy and cowardly reason to simply go with the flow and vote Yes.

On the other hand, we often hear the simplistic refrain 'if you don't understand it, don't vote for it'. That is not a valid basis to vote No. If you don't understand it, then you should find out about it. That is the purpose of this booklet. To give you the information you need to make an informed decision and to be able to defend it – to yourself and to others.

I believe it is not enough that this referendum should fail. In the interests of good governance and a united Australia, it should fail convincingly. And it should do so on the basis of a thorough understanding by all voters of its inherent dangers and weaknesses. It should neither succeed nor fail on the basis of emotional feel-good rhetoric on the one hand, or intuitive distrust on the other.

If its supporters believe it failed because people did not understand the detail, they will simply try again later, and this issue will remain a festering sore in our public discourse for years to come. It must fail on principle, not detail.

Finally, let me say I have no doubt that this booklet will be dismissed by many as simply a polemic – an attack on Aboriginal people. Some of it *is* an attack. But not on the Aboriginal people. It is, in fact, a counter-attack against the constant denigration of Australia as a racist country, and against the Aboriginal grievance industry, which is actually instrumental in holding the most disadvantaged Aborigines back.

# 1

# THE ULURU STATEMENT FROM THE HEART

At the centre of this whole debate is the Uluru Statement from the Heart. This is what it says:

> We, gathered at the 2017 National Constitutional Convention, coming from all points of the southern sky, make this statement from the heart:
>
> Our Aboriginal and Torres Strait Islander tribes were the first sovereign Nations of the Australian continent and its adjacent islands, and possessed it under our own laws and customs.
>
> This our ancestors did, according to the reckoning of our culture, from the Creation, according to the common law from 'time immemorial', and according to science more than 60,000 years ago.
>
> This sovereignty is a spiritual notion: the ancestral tie between the land, or 'mother nature', and the Aboriginal and Torres Strait Islander peoples who were born therefrom, remain attached thereto, and must one day return thither to be united with our ancestors. This link is the basis of the ownership of the soil, or better, of sovereignty.

It has never been ceded or extinguished, and co-exists with the sovereignty of the Crown.

How could it be otherwise? That peoples possessed a land for sixty millennia and this sacred link disappears from world history in merely the last two hundred years?

With substantive constitutional change and structural reform, we believe this ancient sovereignty can shine through as a fuller expression of Australia's nationhood.

Proportionally, we are the most incarcerated people on the planet. We are not an innately criminal people. Our children are alienated from their families at unprecedented rates. This cannot be because we have no love for them. And our youth languish in detention in obscene numbers. They should be our hope for the future.

These dimensions of our crisis tell plainly the structural nature of our problem. This is the torment of our powerlessness.

We seek constitutional reforms to empower our people and take a rightful place in our own country. When we have power over our destiny our children will flourish. They will walk in two worlds and their culture will be a gift to their country.

We call for the establishment of a First Nations Voice enshrined in the Constitution.

Makarrata is the culmination of our agenda: the coming together after a struggle. It captures our aspirations for a fair and truthful relationship with the people of Australia and a better future for our children based on justice and self-determination.

We seek a Makarrata Commission to supervise a process of

agreement-making between governments and First Nations and truth-telling about our history.

In 1967 we were counted, in 2017 we seek to be heard. We leave base camp and start our trek across this vast country. We invite you to walk with us in a movement of the Australian people for a better future.

The first, and critical, thing to note is that the Voice will not be an end to Aboriginal demands. It will not unite us. The Statement talks about reforms. As you can see from the fourth paragraph, these include some notion of a joint 'sovereignty'. And they include a treaty – a treaty between the sovereign nation of Australia and the apparently sovereign 'First Nations'. This is an agenda far beyond providing policy advice. And the Voice is embedded within it – it does not stand alone. It carries with it all these other demands. It is seen, by its proponents, as the means to these other ends.

The claim that Aboriginal 'sovereignty', such as it was, has never been ceded is specious at best. In fact, Aboriginal clans – not nations – never exercised or recognized a concept that we now call sovereignty. That is a complex topic not directly relevant to this debate. However, for clarity I will use that terminology.

Certainly, 'sovereignty' was never ceded via a formal treaty, such as the Treaty of Waitangi in New Zealand. That would have been impossible as there was no overarching Aboriginal authority that could negotiate such a treaty. But, in practical terms, it was ceded on a region-by-region basis, right across the continent, as local

Aboriginal tribes recognised the inevitability of white settlement and accommodated themselves to it – a process known as 'coming in'. This phenomenon, based on self-interest (e.g., a regular supply of food obtained much more easily than foraging or hunting), was described by countless observers, such as Royal Marine Lieutenant Watkin Tench, dating right back to the First Fleet. The celebrated Bennelong was one of the first to make this transition. This was the overwhelming response of Aborigines to colonization, as opposed to the myth, now being peddled, of invasion, of 'wars of resistance' and widespread massacres.

And if you need further convincing, the most explicit act of cession occurred in 1967 when the vast bulk of Aboriginal people enthusiastically lobbied for, and applauded, the amendment to our Constitution that allowed the Commonwealth Government to make laws in respect of Aboriginal people – laws to benefit, not restrict, them. This was an implicit acceptance of the sovereignty, over all Australians, of the Australian Commonwealth.

There is no Aboriginal sovereignty. Aborigines may have title to Aboriginal land, but this does not carry with it any form of sovereignty, any more than you, as a home-owner or farmer, have a sovereignty over your land.

The real purpose behind the Voice, as I will show later, is as a springboard for more radical demands such as a treaty and a form of self-government. If you are sympathetic to the idea of a Voice but find the idea of a separate sovereignty for Aboriginal people –

one section of our people governed by a different set of laws to the rest of us – repugnant, then I hope I can convince you that, whatever its proponents might now claim, this will be the inevitable result of putting the Voice into the Constitution.

'Truth telling' is one of the planks of the Statement. One wonders how many more truths are yet to be revealed. For example, the subject of massacres, and even genocide, increasingly intrudes itself into discussions on the colonization of Australia and is designed to delegitimize our nationhood and to instil a sense of guilt in non-Aboriginal Australians. To soften them up to acquiesce in almost any demand that is now made of them – including treaties and reparation paid to modern Aboriginal Australians – for wrongs committed in the distant past. In September 2022, Prime Minister Albanese recruited this theme in his Voice campaign, when he said, in *The Australian*:

> The Prime Minister said "truth-telling" on the atrocities faced by Indigenous people should be part of learning about Australian history, but it should be done in a way that avoided shaming people of British descent.
>
> "Part of learning about our history is truth-telling as well," Mr Albanese told 4BC radio.
>
> "And the truth is that Indigenous people suffered a lot. Not all, but many did. Massacres occurred. And we need to be truthful about that, not as a way of being shamed but just as being fair dinkum.
>
> "It is the Australian way."

I will have more to say on this subject in a later chapter.

Albanese also, on the night he became Prime Minister, made this issue his very first commitment. But he did not commit to implementing a constitutionally enshrined Voice to Parliament. He committed to implementing, in full, the Uluru Statement from the Heart. With all its attendant baggage – truth telling, treaty and reparations.

This demand for a separate sovereignty is underpinned by the notion of a special spiritual connection with the land, one that is shared by all people of Aboriginal descent. Apparently, you are born with it. You have it no matter how pale your complexion is, nor where you were born, nor at what stage in life you discovered your aboriginality. I will discuss this dubious proposition in my Conclusion.

The Voice, so benign on the surface, is just the thin edge of a wedge that will drive a stake through the heart of the Australian Constitution. A Constitution that was devised as a result of painstaking deliberation and extensive consultation, over a number of years, with *all* the people. It is important to understand that, in 1900, the Colonial Governments included Aborigines among the 'people', and there is ample evidence that they themselves, at least in NSW, Victoria, Tasmania and South Australia, voted for the Constitution.

# 2

# THE PROPOSED VOICE

So, what does this Voice look like?  Here is the draft proposal from the final report of the Indigenous Voice Codesign Committee issued in July 2021.  Its lead authors were Drs Marcia Langton and Tom Calma:

### National Voice overview

### Structure and membership

### 24 Members

- There would be two members from each state and territory, as well as the Torres Strait Islands.
- There would also be a third member for remote representation for NSW, NT, QLD, WA and SA and one member for mainland Torres Strait Islander people.
- Gender balance would be structurally guaranteed.
- Option for two additional members jointly appointed between the National Voice and the Government.

### Membership structurally linked to Local & Regional Voice

**A. Determined by Local & Regional Voice (Default option)**

Local & Regional Voices collectively determine the National Voice members for their state, territory and the Torres Strait. This is the default option.

**OR**

**B. Determined by state or territory representative assemblies**

National Voice members determined by relevant state, territory and Torres Strait representative assemblies, if they are formed by drawing on Local & Regional Voices, where they exist.

**OR**

**C. Hybrid arrangement**

Combination of determining members:

- Determined by special meeting of Local & Regional Voice representatives
- Determined by relevant jurisdiction-level assemblies where these exist (either an elected assembly or drawn from Local & Regional Voices).

## There will be 35 of these Local/Regional Councils:

**Local & Regional Voice**

- Communities across a region decide how best to organise themselves in alignment with the principles and based on their context

- Local communities and groups have clear pathways to participate and connect to their regional structure in a way that works for them – this is referred to as the 'Local & Regional Voice'
- Each region decides how best to draw its voice members (i.e. election, nomination/expressions of interest/selection, drawing on structures based in traditional law and custom, or a combination) and how many voice members there will be
- Existing local/regional bodies (e.g. advisory bodies, statutory and land rights bodies, ACCOs etc.) link in without their roles being duplicated or undermined
- **Minimum expectations**: Meeting Inclusive Participation, Cultural Leadership and Transparency and Accountability principles
- This is the starting point for recognition.
- There is an expectation to meet all principles over time.

**Regional partnership arrangements (e.g. 'partnership table')**

- Local & Regional Voice and all levels of government come together to share advice and decision making on community priorities
- Clear protocols guide this
- Within the scope for Local & Regional Voice, functions may evolve over time, depending on preferences of community and capabilities of all partners

The report tells us that:

> The Local & Regional Co-design Group considers that governments need to provide adequate, secure and long-term

resourcing to enable the effective establishment and ongoing work of Local & Regional Voices.

Resources would cover a secretariat ('backbone') team in each region (to provide administrative, logistical, capability and other support, e.g., data and research capability) to enable local communities and leadership groups to engage in Local & Regional Voice activities, including extensive community engagement and involvement in partnership arrangements with governments.

At the time of writing, some discussion has emerged about whether the Voice should be given the prerogative to provide advice to both Parliament and the executive government or just to the Parliament. As I will discuss later, the prerogative to advise the executive government carries with it substantial risk of costly and disruptive litigation. Because of this risk, a number of constitutional scholars, some of them supporters of the Voice, believe it should be restricted to giving advice to Parliament. PM Albanese has been called upon to amend the referendum question accordingly.

The idea that the Voice would give advice to the executive government was not Albanese's brainchild. He has repeatedly said the Voice is not his proposal. And he will not be permitted by the Referendum Working Group, which is finalizing the question that will be put to the people, to remove that provision. This is because providing advice to the executive government is fundamental to the Uluru strategy, which ultimately sees Aboriginal people exercising political power in their own right, in addition to existing parliamentary structures. Advice to the executive government pervades the 272 page Co-Design Report and it underpins the whole structure of this massively bureaucratic Voice edifice.

Restricting advice to Parliament only, will consign the Voice to being little more than a Constitutionally enshrined lobby group. That is a dangerous enough proposal in any event but the Uluru architects will not settle for that.

As to the provision of advice to government, readers may not be aware that there is no Department of Indigenous Affairs as such. No ivory tower bureaucracy, manned largely by out-of-touch white bureaucrats, ensconsed in Canberra developing policy, drafting laws and overseeing implementation, as we see in most other ministries. The Minister for Indigenous Australians is part of the Department of Prime Minister and Cabinet and exercises her responsibilities through a number of agencies and boards that include:

> Aboriginal Hostels Limited, Anindilyakwa Land Council, Australian Institute of Aboriginal and Torres Strait Islander Studies, Central Land Council, Indigenous Business Australia, Indigenous Land and Sea Corporation, National Indigenous Australians Agency, Northern Land Council, Northern Territory Aboriginal Investment Corporation, Tiwi Land Council, Torres Strait Regional Authority, Wreck Bay Aboriginal Community Council, Aboriginal and Torres Strait Islander Mental Health and Suicide Prevention Advisory Group and Aboriginal Hostels Limited (Board), Australian Institute of Aboriginal and Torres Strait Islander Studies (Board), Central Land Council (Board), Indigenous Business Australia (Board) and the Indigenous Land

and Sea Corporation (Board)

Of the above, the National Indigenous Australians Agency appears to be the lead agency. Its website tells us:

> The National Indigenous Australians Agency was established by an Executive Order signed by the Governor-General on 29 May 2019.
>
> The Executive Order gives the NIAA a number of functions, including:
>
>> to lead and coordinate Commonwealth policy development, program design and implementation and service delivery for Aboriginal and Torres Strait Islander peoples;
>>
>> to provide advice to the Prime Minister and the Minister for Indigenous Australians on whole-of-government priorities for Aboriginal and Torres Strait Islander peoples;
>>
>> to lead and coordinate the development and implementation of Australia's Closing the Gap targets in partnership with Indigenous Australians; and
>>
>> to lead Commonwealth activities to promote reconciliation.

Its staff budget exceeds $1.5 million per annum and last financial year it spent over $2 billion.

In addition to that there is the Council of Peaks, representing some 70 big community-controlled Aboriginal organisations, plus more than 30 land councils, 2700 Aboriginal corporations and 11 federal MPs in our federal parliament.

Voice opponent, Aboriginal Senator Jacinta Price, in an article in *The Australian* on 4 Mar 2023, puts a couple of faces to these bodies:

> Contrary to the argument by voice proponents that Aboriginal Australia has been "voiceless" and needs an overarching entity to hold parliament and executive government to account, [Aboriginal leader, Noel] Pearson himself is among those who have had a seat at the table for decades.
>
> He has been a key player in the Indigenous policy space since the early 1990s. Through the establishment of the Cape York Institute for Policy and Leadership during 2011 to 2016 alone his efforts have attracted more than $47m in government funding for the design and implementation programs to advance communities.
>
> Pearson has had the ear of many prime ministers of both Labor and Coalition governments over the decades. His has been a prominent voice to parliament, despite never taking the opportunity to run for a seat himself.
>
> Another proponent of the voice, Pat Turner, who is currently the head of the Coalition of Aboriginal and Torres Strait Islander Peak Organisations – a body many would consider is a voice to parliament – has also in her own words, "held senior leadership positions in government, business and academia for more than 40 years, and had extensive experience in Aboriginal and Torres Strait Islander affairs".

So, there is hardly a lack of grass roots advice on Aboriginal matters. Nonetheless, the Voice will insinuate itself into the workings of these groups – as well as other Departments such as

Health, Education, Energy and Climate Change – to such an extent they will effectively become part of the government.

And that would make the Voice an Aboriginal-only Parliament.

Before discussing the merits of the proposal, it is worth understanding the Constitution that will be so severely impacted by it.

# 3

# THE AUSTRALIAN CONSTITUTION

The complete Constitution is readily available on-line: *https://ausconstitution.peo.gov.au/.* Everyone should read it, not necessarily to become *au fait* with all its detailed provisions, but in order to understand what it is and, more importantly, what it is not. You are being asked to change the Constitution in a significant way. You should know what it says, *in toto*.

The first thing that you will note is that the Constitution is in two parts. The first is an Act of the British Parliament that established the Commonwealth of Australia in 1901. This is what is sometimes referred to as the preamble. The essence of the Constitution, i.e., the Constitution itself, is that portion which commences at Clause 9 of the Act, titled 'Constitution'.

It comprises:

> Chapter One – The Parliament
>
> > This details provisions relating to the Governor-General, the composition of the Parliament, how members and

Senators are elected and so on. It includes Part V which lists those issues upon which the Parliament may legislate.

Chapter Two – The Executive Government

This short chapter (two pages in all) details how what we call the government is formed.

Chapter Three – The Judicature

This chapter describes the establishment and powers of the High Court.

Chapter Four – Finance and Trade

This chapter covers such details as the Consolidated Revenue Fund, uniform customs, free trade between the States etc.

Chapter Five – The States

This chapter protects the rights of States, prevents them from raising military forces. It establishes that where valid State and Commonwealth laws conflict then Commonwealth law prevails.

Chapter Six – New States

This chapter allows for the creation of new States.

Chapter Seven – Miscellaneous

Chapter Eight – Alteration of the Constitution

The second thing you will notice is that the Constitution says nothing about our history, our values or our aspirations. It says nothing about our rights as individuals. It is, in fact, a very prosaic document. It is not like the American Declaration of Independence. It does not hold any truths to be self-evident. It contains no lofty sentiments. (In fact, neither is the US Constitution like the Declaration. It too is a practical document.)

It is not, as is often claimed, the 'birth certificate' of our nation. If you are looking for a slick but specious analogy, a better choice would be the 'pre-nuptial agreement' of our nation. But, in fact, it is neither of those things.

Firstly, our Constitution is a power sharing agreement between the Commonwealth and the States and, secondly, it is an operating manual for our Parliament. Nothing more. It is, in effect, a contract – one which is subject to the jurisdiction of the High Court. As a contract, it is not an appropriate vehicle for emotional or feel-good rhetoric. That would introduce ambiguities that can, and almost certainly will, have unintended consequences.

Who we are as a nation – our values and aspirations – is reflected in the democratic traditions and institutions we inherited from Great Britain. And, more importantly, in our legislation, which has made us one of the most diverse, tolerant and generous nations on Earth. It is in our legislation that we must look to enrich all the people, to alleviate disadvantage, to unite us and to recognize past injustices. All that we require from the Constitution in this respect is that it offers no impediments to such legislation.

One of the themes that dominates the discussion around the Uluru

Statement is the need to recognize Aboriginal prior occupation of the continent of Australia. The evidence that Australia recognizes this unarguable fact is all around us, as I will elaborate later.

But what would be regarded as the most significant gain for Aboriginal people – a substantive recognition of their prior occupation – would be the Mabo Land Rights decision of 1993. The High Court did not discover native title in the Constitution. It discovered it in the common law we inherited from Great Britain. Common law is extinguished by statute law. The racist Australia that activists such as 'Senator' Lidia Thorpe love to hate, would have legislated native title out of existence. But it did not do that. The Keating government gave it legislative force through the Native Title Act of 1993. As a result of this decision, according to its latest figures, the Native Title Tribunal has determined that 49.3 per cent of the Australian continent now belongs to Aboriginal people. And there are still more claims waiting for another 13.4 per cent of the continent to be formally determined. So, the combined total of land to be defined by the tribunal as belonging, either wholly or partly, to Aboriginal people now amounts to 62.7 per cent of the continent. Only 37.3 per cent of the continent belongs to the rest of us.

This major advance (if you term it that) was achieved without an amendment to the Constitution.

Earlier I adverted to the claim that the Constitution is flawed because it fails to mention the Aboriginal people. You will note that neither does it mention the British or any other people. It simply refers to 'the people'. To accord Aborigines a special mention in the Constitution has implications far beyond merely acknowledgement of their prior occupation of the continent as I will show in the following chapters.

# 4

# INDIGENOUS AUSTRALIANS AND THE CONSTITUTION

It is commonly claimed that the Constitution ignored Aboriginal Australians or that it discriminated against them. That they were not regarded as 'citizens'. This is a myth.

In 1901, indeed until 1949, there were no Australian citizens. We all, including Aborigines, were classed as British subjects. Colonial governments recognized this from the word go. They all made laws in respect of Aboriginal people, mostly designed to protect them. They all appointed Aboriginal Protectors, for instance.

In 1948, the Australian Parliament passed the Australian Citizenship Act which came into force in 1949. The Act stated that all Australian-born and other British subjects resident in Australia for the five years prior to 26 January 1949 were automatically Australian citizens and anyone born in Australia on or after that date was automatically an Australian citizen. There was no exclusion of Aborigines.

A variation of this citizenship claim that is often heard is that, prior to 1967, Aborigines were administered under the Flora and Fauna Act. Minister for Indigenous Australians Linda Burney made this claim when she first entered Parliament. This is an urban myth. There was, in fact, never such a thing as a 'Flora and Fauna Act' in either Commonwealth or Colony/State jurisdictions as even the ABC Fact Check Unit concedes (https://www.abc.net.au/news/2018-03-20/fact-check-flora-and-fauna-1967-referendum/9550650).

This is a complex subject, which is beyond the scope of this book, but it would be fair to say that, despite numerous failures (which have persisted to this day) official policy towards Aborigines was always well intentioned. That they were often confined to reservations in the 19th and early 20th centuries is now a subject of bitter recrimination. Yet it is ironic that this was done largely with the intent of allowing them to preserve their culture – something which is now apparently a major imperative of the activist Aboriginal class. I accept that confining a nomadic people to a limited area was not particularly amenable to the maintenance of that culture. But by the same token, nomadism, fundamental to traditional culture, is no longer practised by the vast majority of Indigenous Australians. And any suggestion now that small, dysfunctional, remote communities – effectively reservations – should be closed down is met with howls of outrage.

Be that as it may, by 1901, although there were certainly elements of what we would now call racism in both the official and private relationships between white and Aboriginal Australians, things had improved for Aborigines to the extent that in New South Wales, Victoria, Tasmania and South Australia, they had been accorded the vote. All adult (21 years) male British subjects, including Aborigines, were entitled to vote in South Australia from 1856, in Victoria from 1857, New South Wales from 1858, and Tasmania from 1896. In South Australia Aboriginal women had the vote in 1895, long before women in the United Kingdom had it.

Think about this. At the same time that the United States of America was engaged in a bloody civil war over the question of slavery, most Aboriginal men in Australia could vote. Before white women could.

When the Constitution came into force in 1901, those voting rights also applied in the Commonwealth. Section 41 of the Constitution made that clear:

> No adult person who has or acquires a right to vote at elections for the more numerous House of the Parliament of a State shall, while the right continues, be prevented by any law of the Commonwealth from voting at elections for either House of the Parliament of the Commonwealth.

So, Aborigines who had a right to vote in the above States, could also vote for the Commonwealth Parliament from the very beginning of the Federation. Furthermore, in order to induce Queensland and Western Australia into extending the vote to their Aboriginal population, the founding fathers included a provision (Section 25) which prevented those States from counting Aboriginal citizens in their population for the purposes of determining how many House of Representatives seats they were entitled to. In other words, if Aboriginals could not vote for the State Parliament, their number could not be used to inflate the population of that State for the purposes of gaining more House of Representatives seats.

The Constitution established a baseline for voting rights, and it was expected that the first Parliament would enact a Commonwealth franchise that would extend the vote, at Federal level, to all permanent residents, including Aborigines. Regrettably, the Commonwealth Franchise Act of 1902 excluded all those Aborigines, i.e., those in Queensland, Western Australia and the Northern Territory, who did not already have the vote by virtue of the provisions of Section 41. It must be said that this was largely at the behest of the Labor Party, and despite the spirited opposition of the Barton government. Labor reasoned that if Queensland and Western Australia did not trust Aborigines to vote for their Parliament, it would be inconsistent with the spirit of federalism to allow them to vote in Federal elections. However much we might now deplore this as 'racist', in 1902, with federalism still so strong, it was not an unreasonable proposition. Interested readers are encouraged to explore the comprehensive coverage of this issue in Keith Windschuttle's *The Break-Up of Australia* published by Quadrant Books.

But the fact remains that the vast majority of Aboriginal Australians who lived within mainstream Australian settlement, i.e., not remote communities, could vote for the Commonwealth Parliament from 1901. They voted for the first Parliament. And there is ample evidence that they voted, in significant numbers, for every succeeding Parliament.

This right, although enshrined in the Constitution, was given practical effect by legislation. As has every initiative that has advanced Aboriginal well-being since then. There has been only one Constitutional amendment that affected Aboriginal people. Let me explain.

In 1949 the right to vote in federal elections was extended, by Commonwealth legislation, to Indigenous residents of Queensland, Western Australia and the Northern Territory who had served in the armed forces, although admittedly they could still not vote in their State/Territory elections.

In 1962, the Commonwealth Electoral Act was amended to extend the right to enrol and vote in Federal elections to all Indigenous Australians, regardless of State law or military service. This included the right to vote in Northern Territory elections. However, enrolment and voting were not made compulsory for Indigenous Australians until 1984. This advance did not require an amendment to the Constitution and it disproves the claim that, prior to 1967, the Constitution excluded Aborigines.

In 1967, a referendum was held to address two questions. The first related to Section 127, which was interpreted as preventing Aboriginal people from being counted in the Commonwealth Census. It is arguable whether or not this was the real intent of that Section (and is beyond the scope of this discussion) but regardless of that, this was how it had been interpreted. As a result of this referendum, Section 127 was repealed. The other, and more significant, question related to the Commonwealth making laws exclusively in respect of Aboriginal people. Prior to this time, only the States could do this, but this, of course, had led to the anomalous situation where Aboriginal people were treated differently in each State. Section 51 of the Constitution was amended to allow the Commonwealth to make special laws for the advancement of Aboriginal people and these laws would take precedence over any conflicting State law. More than 90% of Australians registered a YES vote with all six states voting in favour. Section 51 (xxvi) says:

> The Parliament shall, subject to this Constitution, have power to make laws for the peace, good order, and good government with respect to the people of any race for whom it is deemed necessary to make special laws.

Prior to 1967, this Section specifically excluded Aboriginal people. The original intent of this Section was to give power to the Commonwealth to regulate the conditions under which foreign indentured workers could be allowed entry to the country and under which they might be employed.

In September 2022, in a debate on Sky News, constitutional expert Dr Shireen Morris claimed that the Constitution 'explicitly excluded Aborigines'. In using the word 'explicitly', she can only have been referring to the original Section 51(xxvi) or Section 127 as these are the only sections that explicitly referred to Aborigines. As should now be apparent to readers, Section 51(xxvi) did not exclude Aborigines from the Commonwealth or the Constitution. It merely excluded them from the class of people for whom the Commonwealth could make special laws, because that was the responsibility of the States. As British subjects resident in Australia at the time, Aborigines were subject to every other provision of the Constitution in the same way that white people were. And Section 127, which was repealed in 1967, only constrained government from counting Aboriginal people in 'reckoning the numbers of people of the Commonwealth or a State or other part of the Commonwealth'. It did not exclude them from any other provision of the Constitution. The fact that they were specifically excluded from Sections 51(xxvi) and 127 must necessarily mean they were included in all other provisions.

I have included this anecdote because it highlights the cavalier and duplicitous way in which activists can twist the meaning of words to convey an entirely erroneous impression. Journalist and prominent conservative Voice advocate, Chris Kenny, continues to peddle this myth. When it comes to Aboriginal grievance it is good practice to question every claim that is made.

Want more evidence of this? Well let me introduce Dr Asmi Wood, a Torres Strait Island man and Professor of Law at the Australian National University. In an article in *The Conversation* in March 2023 he asserted, in relation to Section 51(xxvi):

Many judges have taken issue with the "races power". For example,

Justice Robert French has argued the "races power" has recently been used against Aboriginal and Torres Strait Islander peoples.

In other words, the "special treatment" that has been meted out to Aboriginal and Torres Strait Islander peoples has often been painful: the removal of their children, for example, to prevent them speaking their language or practising their spiritual and cultural beliefs.

He provides no evidence whatsoever that, since 1967, any Aboriginal child has been removed for the above reasons. That claim is totally implausible. I will cover the issue of 'Stolen Generations' in Chapter Eleven.

He also adheres to the 'flora and fauna' myth:

The Constitution once also mentioned "Aboriginal natives" for the purposes of exclusion. Section 127 excluded "Aboriginal natives" from the count of the human population and regulated "Aboriginal natives" as fauna – this section was removed in the overwhelmingly supported 1967 referendum.

The 1967 amendment was greeted enthusiastically by Aboriginal people and was regarded as a great advance for them. It now seems somewhat ironic that a people who had conceded, in 1967, that it was in their best interests to have the Commonwealth make specific laws to benefit them, now wish to dictate what those laws should look like. The argument is put, 'if you are going to make laws about us, we should have some say in the formulation of those laws'. If making laws in respect of Aboriginal people is some sort of discrimination, as is implied in this argument, then why not just advocate for the repeal of Section 51(xxvi)? Do we make laws restricting where Aborigines may live, where they may go, who they may marry, where they may work, where they may sit on the bus? Of course not. I will return to this point later.

It is a common misconception that the 1967 referendum granted Aborigines citizenship. That is not true. As I have already shown, Aborigines have always been regarded as either British subjects or Australian citizens – as we all have.

According to a Parliamentary Library Research Paper published in 2012, Section 51 (xxvi) has allowed the Commonwealth government, in the 44 years from 1968, to legislate the allocation of approximately $84 billion to indigenous affairs, i.e., specifically for the benefit of Aboriginal people. Current expenditure is running at about $5 billion per year. This is targeted expenditure. Not every Aboriginal person benefits from this. It does not include general expenditure, such as health and educations services, from which Aborigines also benefit. It is estimated at $27 billion per year. The Productivity Commission reports that:

> Estimated expenditure per person in 2012-13 was $43,449 for Aboriginal and Torres Strait Islander Australians, compared with $20,900 for other Australians (a ratio of 2.08 to 1 — an increase from a ratio of 1.93 to 1 in 2008-09).

I am not saying that this expenditure is unwarranted, just that it belies the suggestion that Indigenous people are second class citizens.

Major milestones of Aboriginal advancement include the following.

In 1971, Neville Bonner was appointed by Queensland Premier Joh Bjelke-Petersen to replace retiring Liberal Senator Dame Annabel Rankin. Bonner was the first Aboriginal to sit in the Australian Parliament. Today there are 11 Aboriginal people in the Australian Parliament.

In 1975, Prime Minister Gough Whitlam negotiated with the owners of Wave Hill pastoral station in the Northern Territory to hand back to the Gurindji people a 3,236-square-kilometre portion of their land.

In 1976, the Aboriginal Land Rights Act, originally drafted by the Whitlam government, was passed by the Fraser government, establishing the mechanism for Aboriginal communities to claim land in the Northern Territory.

In 1990 the Aboriginal and Torres Strait Islander Commission (ATSIC) was created – elected regional councils and a board of commissioners made decisions on policy and funding. ATSIC elections were conducted by the Australian Electoral Commission. It was disbanded in 2005 due to chronic mismanagement.

In 1993, Prime Minister Keating introduced the Native Title Act, establishing the framework for native title in the whole of Australia, giving effect to the High Court Mabo judgement. Since that date, Aboriginal communities have acquired exclusive ownership of roughly 30% of the Australian land mass and have lodged claims for exclusive or non-exclusive ownership of another roughly 40%.

All in all, Australian Parliaments, certainly since 1967, have fallen over themselves to accommodate the aspirations of Aborigines and to overcome the very real disadvantages that a small proportion of them face. Admittedly, their efforts in the latter category seem to have been disappointingly ineffective, but that is not for want of good intention. Some problems are intractable, at least in the short term.

In a general sense Australian governments may have failed the Aboriginal people, but the Constitution, emphatically, has not. And it should not now be tampered with in the name of rectifying a fault that it never exhibited in the first place.

# 5

# WHAT IS THE REASON FOR THE VOICE?

There are two elements to this proposed referendum. The Voice itself and its inclusion in the Constitution. The latter is termed 'enshrinement'. In other words, it's not a practical imperative but an ideological one.

As far as the Voice itself is concerned, its justification hinges on the idea that Aborigines should have a say in the formulation of laws that affect them, and that is the question I will address in this chapter. As I will show, this is a specious argument.

To begin with we need to understand who the Aboriginal people are and what are the laws that are being made in respect of them.

There are three groups of Aboriginal people, each quite different, apart from a common ethnic link.

The first group, and the most populous, are urban Aborigines who live in large cities and towns. In the main they are virtually indistinguishable from anyone else. They are educated, employed and socialized to our modern way of life. They do not live together in enclaves, instead occupying the same spaces as most Australians and other residents. Their aspirations, values and their life challenges mirror those of mainstream Australian society. It is from this group that the vast majority of activists are drawn.

The second group are urban Aborigines who live in smaller towns. Generally, these towns have significant Aboriginal populations, and this group has a tendency to live together in Aboriginal enclaves. They socialize, largely, among themselves. They do suffer a degree of disadvantage, and sometimes racist antipathy. Statistically, they are less likely to attend higher education (which may be symptomatic of the small community), but they are employed in the same proportion as other lower socio-economic groups. They live in well maintained houses, their children go to school, are generally healthy and adequately fed. Much of the disadvantage they may suffer is attributable primarily to their lower socio-economic status, not their race. Included in this group would be communities living in enclaves in large cities, such as Redfern in Sydney. These communities are drawn together not by discrimination but by the common human instinct to socialize with cultural contemporaries.

Then there are the remote and/or tribal Aborigines, and fringe communities in outback towns. These groups tend to be close-knit with less ethnic diversity. They live in communities with high-level family connections and report a lower standard of education than their urban cousins. Given the size and isolation of these communities, they are often unemployed, and practice, to varying extents, aspects of traditional culture. In many of these communities, disease, alcoholism, domestic and sexual abuse are rife. In particular, tribalism is a major inhibitor of progress.

For example, in Aurukun North Queensland, in January 2020 such violence flared up to the extent that 300 of the 1200 residents fled the community. There is a structural problem in Aurukun that embeds the violence as perpetual. The 1200 people within Aurukun Shire are culturally divided into five clan groupings: Wanam, Winchanam, Puch, Apalech, and Sara. Generational vendettas based on "payback" have regularly flared into street fights among fighting aged males from 16 and 49, armed with bows and spears. Aurukun is not alone. Wadeye, in the Northern Territory, is another case.

Obviously, laws that impact on these different Aboriginal groupings will vary significantly. And to suggest that educated urban Aborigines will have a unique insight into the problems faced by dysfunctional remote communities – an insight superior to those of the local community and recognized subject experts – is just fanciful. Remote Aborigines are not disadvantaged, and their communities are not dysfunctional, because of their race. There is a reason Aboriginal society did not develop agriculture, the wheel, pottery, metallurgy, writing or weaving etc, and it is not because they were unintelligent. The achievements of David Unaipon, Reg Saunders and Marcia Langton – to name but a few – attest to that. The reason Aborigines did not advance as other societies did is because their culture – highly collectivist, patriarchal, misogynistic and insular – strongly militated against innovation and change. And it is no co-incidence that the most disadvantaged Aborigines today are those that cling most stubbornly to what little remains of that culture and, indeed, are encouraged to do so. The works of anthropologists Ted Strehlow, Bill Stanner and Paul Hasluck show that genuine traditional culture had died out, and been replaced with a hybrid culture, in most of Australia before federation and in northern and central Australia by the end of World War Two. I will have more to say on this in my Conclusion.

Legislation that impacts the Aboriginal population covers two main types. There is coercive legislation designed to curb dangerous and anti-social behaviour. And there is enhancing legislation designed to advance Aboriginal people in education, sport, employment, health and housing.

Coercive legislation applies only to those communities that are dysfunctional or severely disadvantaged. It affects relatively few Aboriginals – less than 20% of their population.

As far as I am aware, no urban Aboriginal activist has ever had any major, in principle, issues with enhancing legislation that distributes public money to Aboriginal causes, be they substantive – such as guaranteed university places, protection of Aboriginal heritage etc – or symbolic, such as promotion of Aboriginal culture.

No Aborigine is compelled to accept any of this largesse if they find it inadequate or wrongly targeted. But they are free to lobby to have it changed or expanded. They can do this through their

Parliamentary representatives or through their own activist groups. In exactly the same way that, for example, farmers have a say in the formulation of laws that affect them via the National Farmers Federation.

On the other hand, coercive legislation is contentious and should be underpinned by the most rigorous expert advice available. And it should certainly be informed by the people most directly affected by it, i.e., leaders in the communities affected.

One of the most contentious of these was the 'intervention' imposed on certain communities in the Northern Territory by the Howard government in response to the 'Little Children Are Sacred' report. Coercive measures included welfare income management and banning of alcohol and pornography. Measures also included improvements to health and policing. The intervention received mixed reviews from Aboriginal groups but was generally well received by the communities involved, particularly the women.

More recently, the Coalition government instituted a trial of the cashless welfare card in a number of locations not restricted to Aboriginal communities. That has also been contentious, attracting both support and criticism. The Albanese government has since cancelled the cashless welfare card and has supported the NT government in ending alcohol bans. I will talk more about this decision later.

A point to remember is that no Aborigine is compelled to remain in a community, in which restrictions have been imposed, if he/she finds them intolerable. Having said that, I do accept that moving is a last resort and may not be easy.

Legislation that interferes with the lives of Indigenous people certainly requires rigorous planning, including advice from recognized subject experts and the people most affected. But because this coercive legislation is highly targeted geographically and, generally, time constrained, getting such advice is not difficult. The best people to provide an indigenous perspective on such legislation are those living in affected communities and their local elders and Land Council representatives. And, of course, Aboriginal professionals appropriately trained in these matters. And it would be derelict of government not to engage such advice in any circumstances. The existence of the Voice would not absolve it of this responsibility.

However, the further from these communities the source of advice is, the less useful it is likely to be.

Imagine a scenario in which the local community supports something such as an alcohol ban or a cashless welfare card, but the Voice opposes it because it is discriminatory or 'racist'. That is a highly likely result of a national body comprising 24 members, developing advice based on the input from 35 Regional Councils spread across Australia, representing a demographic as widely diverse as the Aboriginal population of Australia. There will inevitably be a diluting or corrupting effect on the advice that originates from the most affected region, by the time it is issued by the national body, which will inevitably be dominated by educated urban activists. And this effect will be magnified by the tribalism I referred to earlier.

What does the government do? Does it accept the advice from the Voice? Does it modify its legislation in some way to placate both sides? Or does it accept the local advice and ignore the Voice, as it should?

Of course, the government is free, in theory at least, to ignore advice from both sources, but the fact is that, in these cases of coercive legislation, the local advice is likely to be more relevant and useful than that from the Voice. In which case, what is the point of the Voice?

Certainly, it will be very effective in lobbying for more enhancing legislation, more university placements, more grants etc, but in the areas where it really matters – on the ground in dysfunctional communities – it will be virtually useless in any practical sense.

At the risk of labouring the point, here are the proposed guidelines for provision of advice, taken from the Codesign Report:

> The Australian Parliament and Government would be 'obliged' to ask the National Voice for advice on a defined and limited number of proposed laws and policies that overwhelmingly affect Aboriginal and Torres Strait Islander peoples. There would also be an 'expectation' to consult the National Voice, based on a set of principles, on a wider group of policies and laws that significantly affect Aboriginal and Torres Strait Islander peoples.

To begin with, it would be a derelict government that did not consult with all relevant groups and agencies on laws that overwhelmingly affect Aboriginal and Torres Strait Islander people. These would be the coercive types of legislation that I have discussed earlier but also would include enhancing legislation which confers benefits on the Aboriginal population, most of which would have been contemplated in the first instance as a result of lobbying by Aboriginal groups themselves. But the wider group of policies and laws that significantly affect them is a very wide ambit, since it could be argued that most laws that impact the entire population may have a particular impact on Indigenous people. Anything to do with finance or taxes for example.

And, secondly, have Aboriginal groups not been providing advice up to now? How did all that enhancing legislation appear? Was it just conjured up by well-meaning white politicians? Aboriginal leader, Warren Mundine, has observed that every time he visits Parliament House, he finds himself tripping over other Aboriginal lobbyists, all busy plying their trade.

Tony Letford, writing in Spectator, tells us:

> Closing the Gap is an organisation mainly funded by various government bodies. According to its website, their objective is to 'enable Aboriginal and Torres Strait Islander people and governments to work together to overcome the inequality experienced by Aboriginal and Torres Strait Islander people and achieve life outcomes equal to all Australians'.
>
> The organisation was 'developed in genuine partnership

between Australian governments and the Coalition of Aboriginal and Torres Strait Islander Peak Organisations' (the Coalition of Peaks), to ensure that 'the views and expertise of Aboriginal and Torres Strait Islander people, including Elders, Traditional Owners and Native Title holders, communities and organisations will continue to provide central guidance to...national governments'. The Coalition of the Peaks is, according to its website, 'a representative body of over seventy Aboriginal and Torres Strait Islander community-controlled peak organisations and members (who are) to be formal partners with Australian governments on Closing the Gap'. The website also claims that 'We have worked for our communities for a long time and are working to ensure the full involvement of Aboriginal and Torres Strait Islander peoples in shared decision-making with Australian governments across the country to improve the life outcomes of our people'.

This is a very worthy aim, and one might reasonably ask why we need yet another organisation to replicate this function.

Why indeed.

Another argument in support of the Voice is that it is a necessary part of 'closing the gap', i.e., eliminating the disparity between the Aboriginal population and the rest of us in respect of a number of metrics e.g., infant mortality, educational achievement, incarceration and so on. The gap is significant, and it is shameful. But what is its extent?

The Aboriginal population of Australia is roughly 800,000 people. Former Labor Minister Gary Johns has shown, in his book *The Burden of Culture* (Quadrant Books), that the genuinely marginalised Aboriginal people – those that are affected by the 'gap' – represent only 20% of this population, i.e., some 160,000 people at most. The other 640,000 are fully integrated into mainstream Australian society and have no need of special legislation. Many of them have only discovered their aboriginality later in life and many of them are the offspring of mixed race families. Aboriginal researcher Suzanne Ingram at the University of Sydney, and others, are concerned that this trend of identifying as Aboriginal, either through being born into a (possibly well to do) mixed race family or through discovering a long lost Aboriginal connection, will see the general Aboriginal population continue to rise to such an extent that it will overwhelm the genuinely disadvantaged population and will distort the statistics relating to the gap. The Aboriginal population has exploded in recent years and can only continue to do so if any admixture of Aboriginal blood qualifies one to be a member. Are all these people to be regarded as a privileged minority in perpetuity?

At the time of writing, Prime Minister Albanese has pointedly refused to commit to legislating the Voice in the event the referendum fails. That is probably a tactical move on his part. Albanese is between a rock and a hard place when it comes to this question. If he says 'yes I will legislate it' many people, who believe the hype that this is about getting the best advice on Aboriginal matters, will think 'well, if that's the case why risk a constitutional amendment. Let's legislate it first and see how it shapes up.' That is certain to weaken the yes vote. On the other hand, if he says 'no', people will realize he's not really interested in getting optimal advice and that this is just a subterfuge for a wider agenda – a 'constitutional recognition' foothold. Which is, in fact, what it is.

Journalist and Voice proponent, Chris Kenny, says:

> ... if you want this device enshrined in the Constitution to ensure Indigenous Australians are recognised in the document, and that all governments must hear their advice, then surely you must accept that the failure of such a referendum would rule out even a legislated voice for some time to come. The will of the people must count for something. Otherwise, the referendum is a farce.

It surprises me that Kenny would take this line. He seems to be saying 'a Voice in the Constitution or nothing'. That suggests to me that his primary reason for supporting this proposal is not so that government can get the best advice possible concerning Aboriginal matters (a doubtful proposition in my view) but that it is primarily about achieving constitutional recognition of Aborigines. A No vote in the referendum does not mean a no vote to the concept of the Voice, just a no to putting it in the Constitution. If the Voice is worth putting in the Constitution (with all the attendant risks) for what it can achieve for Aborigines, then failing that, surely it must be legislated? By conflating two issues – advice and constitutional recognition – its proponents are making a rod for their own back.

Aboriginal leader Noel Pearson, quoted in *The Australian* on 24 January 2023, makes no bones about this:

After the Prime Minister last week refused to rule out trying to legislate the voice if the people voted No at the referendum, Mr Pearson dismissed the idea of establishing an Indigenous advisory body without first achieving constitutional recognition.

"The voice is and was all about constitutional recognition. Whatever was done in the wake of the failure of the voice at a referendum, it wouldn't be the voice," he said. "We'd just probably wind back the clock and go 'the government of the day can decide to establish a completely useless Indigenous advisory body."

He seems to be saying, the Voice will only be effective if it is in the Constitution. On the face of it, that is a nonsensical argument. The only way this would make sense is if being in the Constitution would give the Voice real teeth and could compel the government to not just listen to its advice but also to heed it. And that is what Pearson expects. This, as I will argue later, could be achieved through litigation in the High Court.

This Voice will not be an insubstantial edifice. As we have seen, it will require a secretariat for the National Body and one for each of 35 Regional Councils. They will require premises. There will be salaries for staff, the cost of elections, allowances for delegates, publication of official and promotional material, websites, commissioning of reports and studies, national and overseas fact-finding missions, attendance at international conferences and so on. The cost, however constrained initially, will inevitably blow out. And, significantly, this infrastructure will be replicated at State level as well, providing, if nothing else, a useful source of employment for legions of Aboriginal Australians.

Normally, establishment of such a large bureaucracy would require a cost benefit analysis. Has this been done? I suspect not. We can argue about the details of the Voice and agree to await further clarification, but the one critical detail that is missing is any evidence whatsoever – apart from feel-good rhetoric – that this Voice will improve the lives of any Aborigines, other than those who jump on board what Senator Jacinta Price has described as this 'gravy train'. What compelling difference is there between this proposal and all the other advisory bodies that have gone before, that would convince us to dispense with the tried-and-true notion of 'try before you buy'? I'm talking about 'enshrinement' in the Constitution here, which is the subject of the next chapter.

# 6

# ENSHRINEMENT

If the Voice is to come into existence it must, eventually, be legislated. That could be done in this term of government, given that the Labor government has committed to it, it has the numbers in the House of Representatives and the Greens are likely to support it in the Senate. Many Coalition Members also support it.

If the Voice is indeed an important practical measure that will improve the lives of Indigenous Australians, then why not commence action to legislate it now? Why wait until after a referendum – which is not guaranteed to succeed – to release the form of the Voice and the legislation that will underpin it? Journalist James Campbell asked that question of a newly appointed Labor minister:

> But why, I asked, not legislate a voice first as the last government wanted to do? If it works well the chance of getting Australians to vote to entrench it in the constitution will have improved massively. If it's a fiasco, well, maybe it wasn't a great idea to begin with.
>
> Either way, I said, given history shows that when it comes to any

sort of constitutional change Australians won't touch a pig-in-a-poke, why not try a softly-softly approach?

The answer, it was explained to me, is because Labor's position on this is now effectively in the hands of the Indigenous members of the caucus, and this is what they want.

This makes it clear that Aboriginal Australians already have a pretty effective voice in Parliament. In fact, there are now 11 of them.

Another reason they may resist legislating the Voice first is because the details and costs may prove unacceptable to the Australian people. Once the Voice, in some nebulous form, is in the Constitution, any government will have no choice but to proceed with it in some form or another.

Why not get the Voice operational and see how effective it is before we make it impregnable?

In fact, making it impregnable is the main purpose of this referendum. The fact that the Voice, comprising elected and appointed members from a particular group, derives from a statement that demands recognition of some form of Aboriginal sovereignty, makes it, incontrovertibly, a political entity. Even a caveat that the Parliament is not obliged to accept its advice will not change that. The Constitution recognizes the Commonwealth and the States, of which there are currently six. It does not recognize any other political entity, such as the Territories or local councils, other than the fact that they may exist. It does not recognize the

Loans Council. It does not recognize the Premiers Conference. It does not even recognize the Office of Prime Minister and Cabinet. 'Enshrinement' of the Voice within the Constitution will establish an eighth political entity. Or, to be more precise, a third constitutional entity, alongside the Commonwealth and the States.

Voters must ask themselves if they are happy to accept, in our Constitution, a new political entity, on equal standing with the States. In fact, Voice proponent, journalist Chris Kenny, who was also a member of the Senior Advisory Group of the Voice Codesign process, himself made this point:

> Former prime minister Tony Abbott — a leading opponent of the Voice, to be sure — neatly argues that recognition of Indigenous Australians would not alter the constitution so much as complete it. This is true because the Constitution brought together six groups — the peoples of six colonies — and the people it overlooked as partners or participants were the original inhabitants.

Kenny's justification for supporting Tony Abbott's statement i.e., that Indigenous Australians should have been an eighth partner in the federation, is startling in its naivete – and its potential for mischief. To begin with, the basic premise of Kenny's contention is wrong. It implies that before 1901 Aborigines constituted their own distinct entity within the Australian polity. That is not so. Aborigines, like the colonists, were British subjects under the Crown in the colony in which they resided. They were not overlooked.

Since the Constitution is essentially a prosaic document — a power-sharing contract, if you like – if Kenny's thesis were the acknowledged basis for including Aboriginal Australians in the Constitution, it would necessarily imply that some form of political power resides with them. It would give them the same political status as the six States. If Kenny's logic formed part of the YES case – even if the amendment were not written in those specific terms – that would provide ample and powerful ammunition for an activist High Court to concede political power to Indigenous Australians – power the vast majority of Australians never before envisaged – on the basis that this is what the Australian public really intended (whether they knew it or not) when they voted for the amendment.

But even if the above logic were not explicitly a part of the referendum YES case – even if the justification for putting the Voice into the Constitution were solely to protect it from political emasculation – that would give Aboriginal activists, such as Professors Marcia Langton and Megan Davis, a solid platform to advance a much more radical agenda.

Let me explain. The claim by all proponents of the Voice is that it would give advice only. There would be no compulsion upon the government of the day to accept that advice – it need only consider it. That limitation would, I believe, be essential for a majority of Australians to support the concept of the Voice, whether it be legislated or constitutionally 'enshrined'.

But there is a way that limitation could be compromised.

The Declaration on the Rights of Indigenous Peoples is a resolution passed by the United Nations in 2007. The Australian Government, under John Howard, refused to sign this declaration but, in 2009, the Rudd government formally endorsed it. That endorsement stands to this day, which suggests that there is now bipartisan support for the Declaration. It therefore now, arguably, forms part of our common law.

Article 19 of the Declaration (much of which was drafted by Aboriginal activists Mick Dodson and Megan Davis) states:

> States shall consult and cooperate in good faith with the indigenous peoples concerned through their own representative institutions in order to obtain their free, prior and informed consent before adopting and implementing legislative or administrative measures that may affect them.

'Free, prior and informed consent'. I do not believe a majority of Australians would support such a radical proposal, if specifically asked to do so. But a Voice whose advice is not binding falls a long way short of this demand. It is not what the Aboriginal activists ultimately want. As long as the Voice exists in legislation only, it would be possible to avoid implementing Article 19. But if the Voice ever made it into the Constitution, the matter would be taken out of the hands of the government and placed in the hands of unelected and tenure–secure High Court judges, where those unintended consequences I referred to earlier might come into play.

If my argument sounds farfetched, let me give you one recent example of judicial activism. In 2020, the High Court ruled (The High Court of Australia, 'Thoms v The Commonwealth of Australia', Case B43/2018) that a person of Aboriginal descent, although not born in this country and not a citizen, could not be regarded as an alien under Section 51 (xix) of the Constitution. This was in response to a decision of the Morrison government to deport convicted criminal Brendan Thoms – of Aboriginal descent but *not* born in this country and *not* a citizen – back to New Zealand. Part of the justification for that ruling was that Parliament cannot define the terms in the Constitution. That is the prerogative of the High Court. It seems to me to be an example of the High Court making law. The logic that determined that one class of person i.e., someone of aboriginal descent, is exempt from the commonly accepted definition of an alien as one who is not a citizen, because of his/her putative 'spiritual connection with the land', seems perverse to me as it did to three of the seven High Court judges. The High Court created a new category of non-citizen called a 'belonger'. This case (and a related one – Love v the Commonwealth) is more complex than I have portrayed, but the essential point here is that the High Court has already demonstrated a willingness to make laws that especially favour Aborigines, that regard them as constitutionally distinct from all other Australians.

Back to the Voice. Activists could appeal a law they considered was not based on 'free, prior and informed consent', on the basis that 'enshrinement' of the Voice had given constitutional effect to Article

19 of the Declaration, in that it established a genuine 'representative institution'. They could argue that our obligations under Article 19 over-ride a caveat, inserted into the Constitution *after* the adoption of the Declaration, that advice be non-binding. It is quite possible that the High Court which gave us the Thoms decision, could buy an such an argument and rule that, notwithstanding any caveat in the Constitution, government was bound by its own common law to obtain 'consent' for any law that affected Aboriginal people. It is the policy of the Australian Greens, who now hold unprecedented power in our Parliament, to legislate this Declaration into statute law. That is not out of question. If Labor were prepared to endorse the Declaration, would they hesitate to legislate it if pressed hard enough by the Greens?

This goes to the question of justiciability. Prime Minister Albanese has said on Radio 2GB:

> The Calma Langton [Codesign] report makes very clear that they do not want the body to be justiciable, that is able to go to court to say 'we weren't asked about x policy, we should have been'. That will not be allowed.

Journalist and lawyer Janet Albrechtsen has examined this issue in some depth in a series of articles in *The Australian*. In those articles, available online, she quotes former High Court Justices Kenneth Hayne (a supporter of the Voice) and Ian Callinan (an opponent) who both make it clear that the High Court, not the government, will be the final arbiter on whether or not a matter arising from the Voice is justiciable, i.e., can be appealed in the High Court.

Once the Voice is in the Constitution, Albanese, Calma, Langton etc will have no say in how activists choose to deploy it. I use the word 'deploy' deliberately. It will be a weapon at the disposal of activists who want much more than Albanese envisages. It will be the High Court which decides if something is justiciable, not the government.

I might be drawing a long bow here, but one thing you can be sure of, with the Declaration on the Rights of Indigenous People lurking in the wings, the demands will not cease once, what most Aboriginal activists see as just a first step is implemented.

Proponents of the Voice argue that it must be put into the Constitution to protect it from being disbanded by some future government. Many Australians who might be inclined to support the Voice, will do so in the belief that, at some point when all Aboriginal disadvantage has been eliminated, then it will no longer be needed. If it attracts such public support as is claimed and was working effectively, then it would be a foolish government that disbanded it before its time. But if it were in the Constitution, getting rid of it after its use-by date would be almost impossible. And the same applies if it were found to be dysfunctional (as the Aboriginal and Torres Strait Islander Commission was) or ineffective.

But the real intention of the Aboriginal activists and their supporters is that the Voice should remain for all time. It is a Trojan horse. Or perhaps an analogy that might resonate more, in this day and age, is that it is a piece of constitutional malware.

Aboriginal activists want Parliament to continue, in perpetuity, to make special laws to benefit them, but only on their own terms. Or, at least until they gain their own sovereignty as a separate nation or state within the Federation. The Voice is the first step in corrupting our Constitution to the extent that it can be manipulated by legal and political activists to make it mean whatever they want it to mean.

Professor David Flint, a widely acknowledged expert in Constitutional law, argues that, regardless of the merits of this proposal, it is such a significant change that it requires a more rigorous treatment than the normal referendum process outlined in Section 128 of the Constitution. Such changes are designed to correct some Constitutional anomaly or to include minor provisions required by changed political or social circumstances. But this is such a momentous change – a fundamental restructuring of the Constitution – that it should not be left in the hands of Parliaments and a handful of activists. He proposes the people be brought into the issue from the beginning through the calling of an elected and unpaid constitutional convention. He cited the example of the 1897-1898 federation convention:

> It is highly appropriate to the process for a referendum on the recognition of the indigenous people, that convention be recalled. It is clear that without that elected constitutional convention, federation would probably never have been achieved. The previous constitutional convention held in 1891 was not elected. While it agreed to a Federal Constitution, the six state or then colonial parliaments could not be persuaded to adopt it.

After a call from the people's Corowa conference in 1893, a convention was elected and met in Adelaide in March 1897, then in Sydney in August, and finally in Melbourne in January 1898. In between the sessions there was much consultation, debate in the colonial parliaments and public discussion of the draft Constitution. This was followed by an unsuccessful referendum, the adoption by the Premiers of some amendments satisfactory to New South Wales, and a final series of successful referendums in each of the six colonies.

Indeed, Professor Flint believes that such a convention is overdue, not to consider Aboriginal recognition *per se*, but to review the Constitution overall. He believes that governance is working poorly in Australia, and even the concept of federalism – as envisaged by the founders and approved by the people not only in adopting the Constitution but in refusing to grant changes sought subsequently by the politicians – has been eviscerated by politicians and activist judges.

Rather than 'enshrinement', let's call it what it really is – entrenchment.

# 7

# RECOGNITION OF 'FIRST NATIONS' PEOPLE

The claim is made that recognition, in the Constitution, of Aboriginal people as the original owners/inhabitants of this continent will make them feel empowered and give them confidence to stride ahead into the future. Some will tell you this recognition is purely symbolic. Mostly it is white supporters who push this line. The most influential Indigenous activists reject mere symbolism. They are quite open about the fact that they want some form of self-government. They want their own political power. However, for the moment let's look at the idea of symbolic recognition.

My question is, what would be the game changing factor in this symbolic gesture that would trump all the other gestures and practical actions that have gone before? What is it about a mention in a document, that most people have never read, that would succeed where the gestures and measures outlined below have apparently failed?

Why would not Indigenous people already feel empowered and included when they see their flag flying outside every public building in the land?

Why would not Indigenous people already feel empowered and included when they are acknowledged at every public event?

Why would not Indigenous people already feel empowered and included when they are invited to welcome us to their country at almost every public event?

Why would not Indigenous people already feel empowered and included when they see their culture mandated as a cross curriculum imperative in our schools?

Why would not Indigenous people feel empowered and included when they see their culture front and centre at the opening ceremony of all major sporting events?

Why would not Indigenous people already feel empowered and included when they remember that in 1970 Lionel Rose was named the 9th Australian of the Year, the first of 9 Indigenous people who have been so honoured in the 62 year history of the award? That in 1995, David Unaipon featured on our $50 note? That in 1972 Pastor Douglas Nicholls was knighted and in 1976 became Governor of South Australia?

I could go on, but I'm sure you get my point.

As recently as September 2022, in an interview with Professor

David Flint, former Prime Minister Tony Abbott, who opposes the Voice, expressed his view that there is one final symbolic act of recognition that will make us complete. And that is the insertion of the following amended wording in the 'preamble' of the Constitution:

> Whereas the people ... humbly relying on the blessing of Almighty God, have agreed to unite in one indissoluble federal commonwealth under the Crown ... to create a nation with an Indigenous heritage, a British foundation, and an immigrant character ...

In response to a concern expressed by Flint that this would open the door for activist judges to re-interpret the Constitution in imaginative ways, Abbott said that his very simple wording left little for an activist judge to work with.

In response to that I quote James Allen, Garrick Professor of Law at the University of Queensland, who, in referring in *The Australian* to the Thoms and Love cases I described earlier, observed that:

> Two years ago, in the Love case, on the question of whether a non-citizen person claiming Aboriginal status could be deported, the majority High Court justices used concepts such as "otherness", "deeper truths", "connections (to Australia that) are spiritual and metaphysical" and more of the same to claim that judge-made law that purported to speak in the name of the Constitution now recognises "that Indigenous peoples can and do possess certain rights and duties that are not possessed by, and cannot be possessed by non-Indigenous peoples of Australia" and that

"different considerations apply ... to ... a person of Aboriginal descent".

They did that with our present Constitution *that gives them nothing to work with*.

And further to that, constitutional law, Professor Greg Craven, a strong proponent of the Voice, writing in *The Australian* in the same month said:

The constitutional provisions [of the proposed Voice] would be mechanical, not thematic. They would be very like the 1967 referendum insertions, which in 50 years have never excited the court. *What would be dangerous in the Constitution are broad, sweeping values. This is where amending the preamble is dangerous*.

I think Abbott, for all his good intentions, is likely to be proved wrong in both his fundamental assumptions. This generous act would not be immune to judicial activism, and it would certainly not satisfy indigenous activists. It would not be an end to the demands for constitutional recognition. To them 'constitutional recognition' doesn't mean just getting a mention along with everybody else. They see that as patronizing, which is exactly what it is. What they want is recognition as a distinct constitutional entity.

As I have pointed out earlier, the Constitution is not an appropriate vehicle for symbolism.

The real agenda, hinted at in the Uluru Statement and openly expressed by many of the leading Indigenous activists, is for a separate Aboriginal sovereignty, of equal standing with the sovereignty that already forms the basis of Australia. This would be a recipe for disaster. You would potentially be governed by a different set of laws from your next-door neighbour.

Here is an example that is already in train. The Yuin people of South-Eastern NSW have lodged a land title claim for the entire south coast for NSW from Sutherland to the Victorian border, including the inshore waters out to three nautical miles. One of the things they want is the unrestricted right to fish these waters. At the moment, Yuin people can take fish for consumption without having a fishing licence, but they are governed by bag limits, which are greater than for the general populace (10 abalone vs 2, and 20 fish vs 10). But they can also apply to exceed these limits for 'cultural purposes'.

Yuin man Kevin Mason says he has been fishing in his ancestral waters since he was a boy, providing much needed food for his community on the New South Wales South Coast. "That's our livelihood, it's the life blood of Aboriginal people," he says. "How to feed [mob], that's been handed down to me and I'll hand it down to my next generation." The proponents claim that the Yuin are a traditional fishing community and fishing is an essential cultural imperative for them, which leads one to wonder why Mr Mason has to feed his mob. Why aren't they all doing it?

The proponents of this claim say that if they are successful it will open up commercial opportunities for them. If the claim is successful, it is possible the ruling might allow traditional owners to restrict access to other Australians.

People's freedom to do what they like, or what they are used to doing in the past, is being constrained all the time in the name of the common good. Mr Mason might like to consider that restrictions on his fishing rights are offset by his ownership of a tinnie which considerably enhances his ability to catch fish, and his ownership of a fridge that allows him to store his catch, and that he doesn't have to eat fish every day. When he's not fishing, he can eat a pizza and watch the footy on his flat screen TV, if he so desires. Mr Mason simply wants to have his cake and eat it too.

Some supporters of the Voice, claim that putting it in the Constitution will enshrine recognition in the form of a practical measure and will therefore be more than symbolic. This is a specious argument. Since the Voice can simply be legislated under powers that already exist in the Constitution, and if, according to their logic it would have no teeth (a proposition which I reject), then 'enshrining' it would *ipso facto* be nothing more than symbolism.

And in fact, Aboriginal activists would regard a purely advisory body as no more than symbolism. They want real power in their own right, not power exercised through our existing Parliamentary system.

In 2013, the Commonwealth Parliament passed the Aboriginal and Torres Strait Islanders Recognition Act which recognized their prior occupation of the continent. This Act was intended to kick start the process for a referendum on constitutional recognition. It allowed the Parliament to establish a review for the way forward and allowed two years for this process to commence. That review never took place and was eventually overtaken by the process of establishing the Uluru Statement. A sunset clause in the Act would have seen it lapse in 2018, however it was extended until 2020. It could easily be resurrected in limited form to provide the same official recognition as the 2013 Act, from our foremost Parliament. It would be a foolish government that ever sought to repeal such an Act.

# 8

# RECONCILIATION

Aboriginal activists and their supporters talk repeatedly about the need for reconciliation. The Voice is promoted as a vital part of this process.

When the National Party announced its opposition to the Voice, National's Member Andrew Gee broke ranks with his party and announced he would support the Voice. Gee said that 'although we've come a long way towards reconciliation, we've still got a long way to go' or words to that effect. Which suggests that Gee actually knows what reconciliation looks like. That would make him pretty much unique, at least among white Australians.

What does reconciliation mean and will entrenching this Voice in the Constitution contribute towards it in any meaningful sense?

Other than in a financial context, the word 'reconciliation' has two meanings. You can become 'reconciled to' something, which means you accept the inevitability of what you cannot control. That is the form of reconciliation that Aborigines should embrace if they really want to help that 20 per cent of their population that is still genuinely disadvantaged.

Or you can become 'reconciled with' someone, which means you put away your differences. This implies a compromise – some give and take on both sides.

But the form of reconciliation demanded by the Aboriginal Industry falls into neither category. It is an open-ended process. How do we know what reconciliation looks like? I don't. It seems we will be reconciled with Aborigines when they tell us we are.

There is an organisation called Reconciliation Australia, which describes itself thus:

> We are an independent not-for profit organisation, the lead body for reconciliation in Australia. We promote and facilitate reconciliation by building relationships, respect and trust between the wider Australian community and Aboriginal and Torres Strait Islander peoples.

Here, from the Reconciliation Australia website, is what reconciliation means to them:

> At its heart, reconciliation is about strengthening relationships between Aboriginal and Torres Strait Islander peoples and non-Indigenous peoples, for the benefit of all Australians.
>
> For Aboriginal and Torres Strait Islander peoples, Australia's colonial history is characterised by devastating land dispossession, violence, and racism. Over the last half-century, however, many significant steps towards reconciliation have been taken.

Reconciliation is an ongoing journey that reminds us that while generations of Australians have fought hard for meaningful change, future gains are likely to take just as much, if not more, effort.

In a just, equitable and reconciled Australia, Aboriginal and Torres Strait Islander children will have the same life chances and choices as non-Indigenous children, and the length and quality of a person's life will not be determined by their racial background.

Our vision of reconciliation is based and measured on five dimensions: historical acceptance; race relations; equality and equity; institutional integrity and unity.

Torres Strait Islander children will have the same life chances and choices as non-Indigenous children. There is a fundamental flaw in that statement. Aboriginal and Torres Strait Islander children already have the same life chances and choices as non-indigenous children. And the length and quality of person's life is not determined by their racial background. Aboriginal disadvantage, where it exists, is due, not to a racist or uncaring Australia, but to adherence to a culture that is not fit for purpose in a modern community. Aboriginal children are not less educated because of lack access to a school but because their parents and elders do not insist that they attend school regularly. They are not sexually abused because of their race, but because it is tolerated by their 'culture'. They do not die disproportionately in infancy because of their race but because, for example, their mothers inflict foetal alcohol syndrome upon them, or are malnourished, or are beaten by their partners during pregnancy.

And it is worth remembering that the vast bulk of the children in the 800,000 Aboriginal population do not suffer this disadvantage.

Here are the bullet points for all five dimensions. My comments are interposed:

> Race Relations
>
> All Australians understand and value Aboriginal and Torres Strait Islander and non-Indigenous cultures, rights and experiences, which results in stronger relationships based on trust and respect and that are free of racism.
>
> Goal: Positive two-way relationships built on trust and respect exist between Aboriginal and Torres Strait Islander and non-Indigenous Australians throughout society.
>
> Action: Overcome racism

Overcome racism? True racism, i.e., the concept that one race is morally or intellectually inferior to another, exists in all societies – both coloured and white – but its extent in Australia is massively overstated. The definition of 'racism' is now a moveable feast. In the minds of many activists, being white is synonymous with being racist, so this is a determinant of reconciliation that is never likely to be achieved.

> Equality and Equity
>
> Aboriginal and Torres Strait Islander peoples participate equally in a range of life opportunities and the unique rights of Aboriginal

and Torres Strait Islander peoples are recognised and upheld.

Goal: Aboriginal and Torres Strait Islander Australians participate equally and equitably in all areas of life – i.e. we have closed the gaps in life outcomes – and the distinctive individual and collective rights and cultures of Aboriginal and Torres Strait Islander peoples are universally recognised and respected. Aboriginal and Torres Strait Islander people are self-determining.

Action: Renew focus on Closing the Gap

What are the 'unique rights' of Aboriginal and Torres Strait Islanders? What rights do they have that the rest of us do not possess? When Aborigines have their own parliament and are governed by their own rules, will that mean we are reconciled? At the moment we are divided politically into the Commonwealth, the six States and two Territories. Where responsibilities are not shared between the two levels of government, laws between the States can diverge. But where responsibility is shared, Commonwealth law overrides State law so that, at a national level, there is one law for all of us and we are all equal before it. Once Aborigines have a form of self-government, as espoused in the above ambition, we will have two classes of citizens. One law for them, one law for us. That is not a recipe for national unity.

Institutional Integrity

The active support of reconciliation by the nation's political, business and community structures.

Goal: Our political, business and community institutions actively support all dimensions of reconciliation.

Action: Capitalise on the RAP Program to create a wider range of opportunities for Aboriginal and Torres Strait Islander Australians.

Let me translate the 'action' plan: blackmail woke corporations to flush shareholders money down the toilet in devising programs and jobs to make otherwise unemployable people feel good about themselves.

Unity

An Australian society that values and recognises Aboriginal and Torres Strait Islander cultures and heritage as a proud part of a shared national identity.

Goal: Aboriginal and Torres Strait Islander histories, cultures and rights are a valued and recognised part of a shared national identity and, as a result, there is national unity.

Action: Achieve a process to recognise Australia's First Peoples in our Constitution.

How much more recognition do they need – for a primitive and not-fit-for-purpose culture and a history of violence, cannibalism, infanticide and superstition – above and beyond the incorporation of Aboriginal themes in every facet of our lives at almost every moment of the day?

Historical Acceptance

All Australians understand and accept the wrongs of the past and their impact on Aboriginal and Torres Strait Islander peoples.

Australia makes amends for past policies and practices ensures these wrongs are never repeated.

Goal: There is widespread acceptance of our nation's history and agreement that the wrongs of the past will never be repeated—there is truth, justice, healing and historical acceptance.

Action: Acknowledge our past through education and understanding.

How much further do they want to penetrate our education system beyond the fact that an Aboriginal perspective is mandated as a cross curriculum priority for all subjects? That, in some schools, children are being taught, for example, Wiradjuri rather than becoming proficient in English?

So far, non-indigenous Australia has done all the reconciling — witness the ubiquity of the Aboriginal flag, the constant refrains of 'we acknowledge the traditional owners', the Aboriginal domination of the opening ceremonies of all major public events, the Aboriginal-only study grants and job placements, the constant, and patronising deferral to Aboriginal 'deep spirituality' and 'connection to country', the relinquishment of 60 per cent of our land mass to some form of native title, and so on almost ad infinitum.

It's time for the Aboriginal people to throw off the shackles of the Aboriginal Industry and do some reconciling 'to' the fact that the vast majority have never had it so good and would not have a fraction of their current lifestyle under traditional culture.

Aboriginal activist Noel Pearson is quoted in *The Australian*, in January 2023, saying he fears reconciliation could be lost "forever" if the Voice referendum was to fail. That sounds more like blackmail than any attempt to forge national unity.

Our path to reconciliation is like the yellow brick road. When we get to the end, we will find it is a chimera, at least as far as national unity is concerned. We will have truth telling thrust down our throats, a treaty forced upon us, and massive reparations paid out.

Aboriginal people may regard the colonization of Australia as a crime, but the fact is it occurred generations ago and it cannot be turned back. What emerged from that traumatic process is one of the most democratic, prosperous and stable nations in the world, in which the vast majority of Aboriginal people thrive along with the Australian people at large. Perhaps the onus is on them to reconcile themselves to that reality and to accept all the benefits that flow from it, as in fact, most of them do.

# 9

# DIVIDING US BY RACE?

Opponents of the Voice, notably Andrew Bolt, claim that the Voice proposal, if incorporated into the Constitution, will divide us by race. Bolt is supported by many other commentators. On the face of it, this seems unarguable. Many of the laws that are potentially subject to consideration by the Voice are made under the power given to the Commonwealth under Section 51 (xxvi) viz., to make laws … with respect to the people of any race for whom it is deemed necessary to make special laws.

Chris Kenny argues that the Constitution already divides us by race:

> Perhaps the most prevalent, damaging, and deceptive critique of the voice is that it splits the nation on race. This is a perverse argument, dressing up a reform aimed at removing racial discrimination and disadvantage as divisive.

> We cannot close the gap – the difference in life outcomes between Indigenous and non-Indigenous Australians – without recognising race. Race has been in the Constitution from the start, and the Constitution already gives the federal government

the power to make laws specifically for Aboriginal people – that was the power the nation backed in the 1967 referendum.

But that provision was enthusiastically adopted by the vast majority of Australians, including Aborigines, and was designed for the benefit of Aboriginal people. In 1967, the power to make laws for the benefit of Indigenous people was predicated on the belief that such laws would help overcome their disadvantages and allow them to participate fully in the life of the Nation – as citizens equal, not only before the law, but in terms of personal development. It simply extended to the Commonwealth, power that had resided solely with the States up until that time. It was not intended, certainly by the vast bulk of the Australian people, that such powers were intended to accord Aboriginal people a special place in our polity.

Chris Kenny says:

> To put all this into perspective it is worth imagining this had been proposed as part of the 1967 referendum – that the Constitution was to be amended so the federal government would have the power to make laws about Indigenous people but, in doing so, would be compelled to consult them. It is hard to imagine that such an addition would have been controversial; it would have seemed logical and still would have passed. In essence, that is all that is being advocated now.

That is at least arguable, but the claim is disingenuous because the basis upon which the public supported the 1967 referendum was, as I have explained above, quite different to what is now being proposed. There is an undercurrent in this debate that Section

51(xxvi) is discriminatory and was somehow imposed upon Aboriginal people against their will. That is not true, as I have explained above.

Andrew Bolt, and others, do not maintain that this proposal is racist based purely on the idea of giving advice to the Parliament. All communities have a right to proffer advice and lobby for their own interests. They do this by establishing and funding their own special interest groups such as, say, the National Farmers Federation. If this proposal were limited to a legislated voice funded from the public purse, that would be a privilege denied all other Australians, but it might be justified under Section 51 (xxvi).

Putting the Voice in the Constitution goes a long way beyond this, because it establishes Aboriginal Australians as a distinct group of people who are afforded a special status, based not on needs but on the fact that some of their ancestors were here before 1788. That these ancestors suffered cultural disruption – sometimes extreme – is a regrettable fact of history, but the truth is that the vast bulk of Aboriginal Australians are immensely better off thanks to colonization. Most of them owe their existence to it.

Arguing whether this division is based on race or some other classification (e.g., historical association) is probably semantics. The fact is, if the concept of a separate sovereignty (for which this Voice is just the first step) comes to fruition, there will be a division between two classes of citizen, based not on need but on ancestry. And as far as recognition in the Constitution is concerned, the same is true. In that sense it would be equally inappropriate to symbolically recognize descendants of First Fleeters, or pre-Federation settlers, or convicts, all of whom are part of our history. Putting Aborigines into the Constitution as a distinct group of people, rather than individuals like the rest of us, creates a special class of people with distinct rights, particularly if this leads to treaties and any form of self-government. This will not be a bunyip aristocracy but a legislated one. But this new class of citizen will come from only one race and there is no way someone not of that race can aspire to it. So, the practical effect is that we will be divided by race. That said, I believe it is ill-advised to apply the term apartheid to this situation. That is the same hyperbole that conservatives decry when those of the Left liken right-wing politicians to fascists or nazis.

# 10

# IS THE VOICE A THIRD CHAMBER?

Former Prime Minister Malcolm Turnbull called this Voice a third chamber of Parliament and he is supported in that contention by former Prime Minister Tony Abbott, who, incidentally, supports symbolic recognition.

Proponents of the Voice deny this by pointing out that the advice from the Voice would not be binding on government. Chris Kenny says:

> The recommendations of an Indigenous voice would carry great political weight, of course, but no constitutional power.

They set great store by this assertion but, as I have agued earlier, it is by no means certain that this would continue to be the case. And carrying 'great political weight' can be a two-edged sword, given the propensity for modern governments to succumb to woke populist causes, irrespective of the consequences. What chance a Labor/Greens government (or even a Liberal one for that matter) accepting flawed advice rather than provoke a fight with the vocal activist class, given special Constitutional status and brandishing the provisions of the Declaration on the Rights of Indigenous Peoples? Odds on, I would think.

The Albanese government decision, which I adverted to earlier, to scrap the cashless welfare card and support the removal of alcohol bans in the Northern Territory is a perfect example of this prediction. The government ignored the advice of two Northern Territorian Aboriginal parliamentarians, Senator Jacinta Price (CLP) and MP Marion Scrymgour (Lab) against this decision, on the basis of the need to 'empower' Aborigines rather than 'patronize' them. If 'empowering ' Aboriginal people is the answer then we might as well remove Section 51(xxvi) from the Constitution altogether.

As a result of the Albanese government decision to remove the cashless welfare card and support the removal of alcohol bans, alcohol fuelled violence in Alice Springs has exploded to such an extent that the mayor has called for Federal intervention. Voice advocate Chris Kenny argues that this proves, or at least supports, the need for the Voice. He says the Albanese government ignored the grassroots advice – advice that Kenny fully agrees with – from two local Aboriginal parliamentarians and accepted contrary advice from urban Aboriginal activists, but that if that advice had come from the Voice, the government would have accepted it. That may be true, but it is highly unlikely such advice would have emanated from the Voice, since it will inevitably be dominated by the very same activists that supported elimination of the cashless welfare card and the alcohol bans.

The proposal is that the members of the national Voice would be appointed by the Regional Councils, which themselves choose how they will select their members – election, nomination/expressions of interest/selection, drawing on structures based in traditional law and custom, or a combination.

Journalist Paul Kelly, writing in *The Australian* noted that:

> Direct election [for the National Voice] was rejected given problems confirming indigeneity and the risk of a low voter turnout.

So how representative is the national Voice going to be? And, if there is a risk of low voter turnout, just how important can this Voice be to the majority of Aboriginal or Islander Australians? Is it going to be the preserve of a minority of noisy activists?

Which raises the question of who may stand for election or appointment and who may vote. Who is an Aborigine or Torres Strait Islander? The accepted definition, for the purposes of qualification for government benefits, is in three parts: they must be of Aboriginal or Torres Strait Islander descent, they must identify as such and they must be accepted as such by the community in which they live. And therein lies a problem. One would think that the most important of these criteria would be the first. Without that foundational qualification, the second two – identification and acceptance – are virtually meaningless. And yet the first is routinely overlooked because to demand proof of descent, such as a DNA test, is regarded as demeaning or racist. This has allowed dubious claims of Aboriginality to flourish.

Author Bruce Pascoe is just one example. Pascoe claims to have Aboriginal descent from no fewer than three tribal groups in NSW, Victoria, and Tasmania. The Victorian and Tasmanian groups have denied his claim, but the Yuin people of NSW have accepted him as one of them. As a result of his identification, Pascoe has sold hundreds of thousands of copies of his book *Dark Emu*, has been showered with literary awards established for Indigenous authors and has been variously honoured by Aboriginal organisations. And yet his documented ancestry has been shown to contain no Aboriginal antecedents. Pascoe has consistently refused to address the disparity between the official record and his own claims. Pascoe is not alone.

Even Aboriginal academics have identified this as a problem. Victoria Grieve-Williams, a Warraimaay historian from the NSW mid-north coast, said:

> In Australia the race shifting phenomenon is pervasive and well recognised by Aboriginal people. The statistics show that the increase is not natural, but it remains a difficult conversation for Australians to have. The race shifters hold the power, they stifle debate and resist scrutiny in various ways, including attacking Aboriginal people who ask who they are in our cultural terms. They tend to be urban-based, clustered in southeast Australia, and raised with all the privilege of being white.

The above discourse intimates that even some people who can

claim a modicum of Aboriginal ancestry may not be welcome in the Voice process. There is every chance this third chamber will include people who have no right to be there. Weeding out the imposters is likely to be costly and divisive, involving protracted court battles.

Former High Court Justice Ian Callinan has highlighted another possibility that would render this body even less effective than I have previously postulated. He asks how long would it be before this Voice was infiltrated by the mainstream political parties, particularly the Greens, as has happened across the board with local councils. It is not hard to imagine a scenario in which a Greens component of the Voice could recruit Aboriginal culture to conduct lawfare against important resource projects, as they have already done in relation to the Santos gas field projects in the Torres Strait and Narrabri.

Regardless of that there is another aspect to this 'third chamber' claim. Tony Abbott says:

> Even though this voice would notionally be advisory, the concept
> of an elected body formally to adjudicate on all matters before the
> parliament impacting Aboriginal people effectively constituted
> – said then PM Malcolm Turnbull – a third legislative chamber.
> Because, in practice, almost nothing could be considered by the
> parliament without the prior deliberation of the voice, he was right.
> And because our system is already logjammed, with governments
> having to pass all legislation through a Senate they don't control,
> and often enough having to work with contrary state governments

too, how was yet another legislative complication going to help?

Abbott clearly believes, as I have argued earlier, that the Voice, legislated or constitutionally 'enshrined', will be ineffective.

The wording of the proposed referendum question is that the Voice 'may make representations to Parliament and government'. So clearly it will not be just a reactive body providing input into proposed legislation. It goes well beyond the mantra of 'if the government is going to make special laws for us, it's only right that we should have a say about those laws'. It will develop its own agenda in competition with that of the agencies of the Minister for Indigenous Australians. What will start out as a large bureaucracy will quickly morph into an even bigger one.

On 20 Feb 2023, Professor Greg Craven, a fervent supporter of the Voice, finally conceded that the prerogative for the Voice to make representations to the government, rather than just to the Parliament, could result in High Court litigation, along the lines I have earlier suggested. If the Constitution decrees that the Voice may make representations to the government, the High Court will rule that it is incumbent upon the government to hear those representations. A fractious Voice could flex its muscles by delaying formal provision of such advice on legislation it opposes until the government agrees to some, or all of, its demands. In this way it would be analogous to a cross bench. Contrary to the assertions of Prime Minister Albanese, the Voice would indeed have teeth.

The Voice is, undoubtedly, a parliament, even though it may not originate legislation. And parliaments are famous for not delivering optimum outcomes but compromises. It will not content itself with proffering advice. What it will deliver are policy demands aimed at entrenching Indigenous privilege – even up to a separate sovereignty – not targeted advice on specific legislation. Through time it will become recognized as a *de facto* Indigenous parliament – it may even come to be called that. So, it is by no means a stretch to call it a third chamber of Parliament.

# 11

# MUST WE ATONE FOREVER?

We now come to the subject of 'truth telling'. Much of the discussion around the idea of constitutional recognition involves demands for reparations for land dispossession and massacres, for the Stolen Generations and even for 'genocide'. These issues are used, both explicitly and subliminally, to buttress the case for the Uluru Statement. For the Voice, for treaties and for 'truth telling'. In this chapter I will argue that much of this rhetoric is overblown.

The colonization of the Australian continent was a traumatic and damaging event for the Aboriginal people of the time. Almost alone in the world, they had maintained a stone age culture virtually unchanged for thousands of years. That was not because their culture was inherently superior or more desirable but because they had been shielded from the evolutionary cultural influences (invasion, trade etc) of surrounding societies. That situation was never going to endure. Change was inevitable. Whether the modern world intruded into the continent by later invasion or simply contact through trade, the resulting encounter with the outside world was going to be more traumatic than it was in 1788. For example, former Greens 'Senator' Lidia Thorpe enjoys a life immeasurably better than that she would have, had the colonization that she so deplores not occurred. Life for Aborigines before colonization was by no means idyllic. And by the way, Thorpe would have been very quickly put in her place by traditional Aboriginal culture in 1788.

Let me begin with the Stolen Generations. We hear the term all the time but how many people understand what it really means? Well, what it means is what the Report of the National Inquiry into the Separation of Aboriginal and Torres Strait Islander Children from Their Families, and its shorter version 'Bringing them Home', says it means. And, essentially, that is that between 1910 and 1970, 45,000 to 50,000 Aboriginal children were permanently removed from functioning families with the aim of eliminating Aboriginality. The co-author of the report, Sir Ronald Wilson, described this as genocide. That has since been taken up with gusto by much of the activist class, both black and white.

Undoubtedly many Aboriginal children were removed into care between 1910 and 1970. This was done for the most obvious of motives. All of these children, the vast majority of them of mixed race, were in danger of abuse or neglect in their original families or communities. In many Aboriginal clans, half-caste children were not welcome. In many cases, children were given into care by their parents. In many cases, children were apprenticed or put into domestic service to enhance their prospects of living a healthy and fulfilling life. None of these removed children (wards) were ever prevented from returning to their families, if they wished to do so. It was not done to 'breed out' Aboriginality, as is claimed by some.

Following the release of the Stolen Generations report individual claims for compensation were lodged in Australian courts. As at 2022, only one of these has been successful. In 1957, one year old Bruce Trevorrow was taken into care for being neglected and kept from his family for a period longer than necessary, *against SA government policy*, by an over-zealous bureaucrat. Trevorrow was awarded $525,000 compensation. No other individual claims have been successful, because the claimants were all found to have been removed into care in order to protect them or because they were abandoned or orphaned. Because of the paucity of genuine cases of 'stealing', government policy at all levels has now been to make blanket awards to groups of claimants, many of whom were not removed themselves but are descendants of those who were and now claim to be suffering 'inter-generational trauma'. The Stolen Generations, and associated claims of genocide, are a myth, as historian Keith Windschuttle has comprehensively demonstrated in Volume Three of his monumental work *The Fabrication of Aboriginal History*, published by Quadrant Books. In particular, Windschuttle has shown that the claim of numbers as high as 50,000 children removed is totally unsustainable. The true figure is closer to 9,000.

This myth is now so firmly entrenched into our national psyche that it is having horrific unintended consequences. Aboriginal children victims of of sexual and physical abuse and neglect are being left in dysfunctional families and communities rather than being safely placed with any family or agency that has the means to care for them, rather than risk another 'stolen generation'.

And now to massacres. Undoubtedly, there were many Aborigines killed in clashes with settlers. And there were massacres. The University of Newcastle maintains a Massacre Map which shows the location and provides details of 416 frontier massacres which resulted in the killing of 11,174 Aborigines between 1788 and 1930. This is a highly emotive topic and engenders strong feelings of guilt on the part of white Australians and strong feelings of injustice on the part of Aboriginal and Islander Australians. It has connotations of genocide and forms one of the bases for claims for reparation.

This 'massacre' narrative is also used to bolster the meme, that I referred to, and refuted, in Chapter One that Aborigines never 'ceded sovereignty' – that they fought a long, sustained and continent-wide war of resistance.

However, not every killing of Aborigines qualifies as a massacre. The Massacre Map project defines a massacre as the deliberate and unlawful killing of six or more undefended people in one operation. The problem with these figures is that they are not sustainable under critical examination.

I have identified one particularly egregious example of dubious scholarship. This is the Tambo Crossing massacre of 1843/4.

The website entry states that between November 1843 and June

1844, settlers massacred 70 Aborigines at Tambo Crossing in eastern Victoria. The original source for this is attributed to Aboriginal Protector George Augustus Robinson who travelled through that area in 1844. In fact, Robinson recorded that this incident was a massacre of Aborigines by an opposing tribe. But historian Peter Gardner managed to interpret Robinson's report as some sort of code to cover up that this was actually a massacre by settlers. I have covered this incident in some detail in my book *Bitter Harvest – the illusion of Aboriginal agriculture in Bruce Pascoe's Dark Emu.*

I am not arguing that massacres did not occur. They did. The most notorious and well known was the Myall Creek massacre of 1838 in which a group of 12 settlers massacred, without any provocation, 28 Aborigines. Seven of those perpetrators were tried, found guilty and hanged. Not a perfect outcome because the remaining five escaped justice. But it illustrates that colonial governments did not turn a blind eye to atrocities, although it is true that they often found it difficult to secure convictions.

What we owe Australians of Aboriginal and Islander descent is respect, and that we do everything we can to bring them all to a standard of living that we all aspire to. This generation does not owe reparations to current Aboriginal people for wrongs committed against their ancestors. We do not owe reparations to them for depriving them of a lifestyle that very few would elect to return to, given the choice.

Germany and Japan committed unspeakable atrocities in World

War Two. These atrocities – systemic and on a vast scale – were committed within living memory and affected people still alive today. And yet we do not demand that modern day Germans and Japanese should pay reparations to us.

# CONCLUSION

Many supporters of the Uluru Statement, e.g., Chris Kenny, speak only of the Voice. For example, in September 2022, writing in *The Australian* Kenny said:

> The Constitution is a practical rule book for the power relationships between the states that make up our federation. But it left out the original inhabitants.

This again highlights that what the Aboriginal activists are seeking, and what Kenny is implicitly endorsing on their behalf, is not 'recognition' but political power. And they want it out of proportion to their numbers.

But the Voice is just one element of the Statement, which Prime Minister Albanese on his first day in office promised to implement. Let me return to the Statement. One of its demands is:

> We seek constitutional reforms to empower our people and take a rightful place in our own country. When we have power over our destiny our children will flourish. They will walk in two worlds and their culture will be a gift to their country.

This does not refer to overcoming disadvantage and dysfunction in Aboriginal communities. It does not refer to 'having a say in laws made about us'. What it means is 'making our own laws about us'.

'A rightful place in our own country' does not mean being citizens equal in all respects to any others. It means a 'special' place.

'Walking in two worlds' does not mean embracing both traditional and modern culture, as citizens in a single country. It means the development of a new hybrid culture that combines elements of traditional Aboriginal lore and the benefits of modern society in a system of governance that will apply only to aboriginal people. Needless to say, this nirvana will be propped up by streams of revenue from the rest of us.

Kenny never talks about treaties and truth telling. Neither do any of the other high-profile proponents of the Voice, such as Professor Marcia Langton – at least not in their public utterances about the Voice.

Make no mistake. As I opined earlier, the Voice is the thin edge of the Aboriginal sovereignty wedge. I also described the Voice as a parliament, if not in name then certainly in nature. And among its first tranche of 'advice' will be demands for treaties and truth-telling. Activists have been quite up-front about this.

And if you think I am overstating this, you have only to look no further than Victoria which has established its own First Peoples Assembly. Their big agenda is not advice to government but what they call 'Treaty'.

> The Assembly has negotiated for the Government to give up some of its power by agreeing to establish an independent Treaty Authority that sits outside of the usual government bureaucracy.

This independent 'umpire' will be grounded in our culture, lore and law, and will facilitate negotiations and help resolve any disputes that arise.

The journey to Treaty mustn't be constrained by colonial concepts, and we need an independent 'umpire' that our people can have confidence in. That's why the agreement we secured is to establish a Treaty Authority that is completely independent from government – it won't report to a Minister and its funding will be insulated from the usual political cycles.

The Authority will be led by First Peoples and grounded in our culture, lore and law.

An independent panel – to be agreed to by the Assembly and the Government – will appoint the Members of the Treaty Authority following a public call for nominations. All Members will be First Peoples.

"This is about stepping outside of the colonial system. We've said to government, if you're serious about Treaty, you'll do it our way, and to their credit, that's what they're doing. This is decolonisation in action." - Marcus Stewart, Assembly Co-Chair.

'You'll do it our way'. Does that sound like reconciliation to you? To me, it sounds rather more like a surrender document than a treaty.

And further:

Treaty must bridge the economic divide caused by dispossession and the Assembly has negotiated the establishment of a First Peoples controlled and managed Self-Determination Fund.

The Self-Determination Fund will do two key things. It will enable Traditional Owners to enter Treaty negotiations with the Government on a more level playing field. It will also empower our communities to build wealth and greater capacity for future generations.

"Yes, we want to enjoy, celebrate and share our culture, but treaty needs to be more than that. It also needs to deliver to our people the economic independence required to achieve self-determination."
- Marcus Stewart, Assembly Co-Chair.

The Victorian government has already provided $65 million for this purpose. We don't know the complete list of demands that will make but it will certainly include reserved seats in the Victorian Parliament.

Incidentally, Marcus Stewart, who has emerged as the new spokesman for the Referendum Working Group, traces his Aboriginality to his great great grandfather, John Franklin, who was orphaned at 4 or 5 years of age, was brought up by a settler family, married a white woman, was granted land by the Victorian government, worked hard and lived life as a respected member of the Yea community until his death in 1921. His story is a fascinating and, indeed, uplifting one. You can read it online. John Franklin did not live life as a victim of white colonialism, and it is hard to see how his great grandson can justifiably claim any such status.

Given the above, do you imagine for one moment that the activists behind the national Voice will be content with providing advice on laws that affect Aboriginals? They have already told us that a treaty (and, no doubt, a self-determination fund) is the ultimate objective, and the Voice is one enabling mechanism. It seems we will have treaties between the Aboriginal community and the rest of us at both State and Federal level.

In fact, the Albanese government has already unwittingly signalled its intention in this respect. In January 2023, former Greens Senator Lidia Thorpe, said she would not support the Voice unless it could be guaranteed that it would not cede Aboriginal sovereignty. The Albanese government rushed to reassure her, as reported in *The Australian*:

> The Albanese government has published a summary of legal advice from constitutional experts who say there is no basis to claims from the far left that an Indigenous voice will cede sovereignty.

The fact that, rather than quash the idea of Aboriginal sovereignty altogether, the Albanese government accepts it, tells you that this is part of the plan. Although the government is careful not to say so explicitly. They are not telling us the full story up-front.

Albanese's expert panel is correct on this point. Once the Voice is in the Constitution, far from ceding Aboriginal sovereignty, it will enhance the notion. I argued earlier that whatever form of 'sovereignty' remained to the Aboriginal community, it was finally ceded in 1967. But that does not mean the High Court could not restore it. If a Voice is entrenched in the Constitution – put there on the basis that it forms part of the Uluru Statement which includes demands for treaty and some form of sovereignty – it would be very easy for an activist Court to accommodate this divisive aspiration.

Prime Minister Albanese says that the Constitutional provision defining this Voice needs only to outline the principle and that it is up to Parliament to fill in the details when it legislates the Voice. You might imagine that governments would be very reluctant to concede any of their power to another body – it is not normally in their nature – but the example of what the Victorian government has already done suggests that when it comes to Aboriginal grievance, all bets are off. This is particularly true of a government beholden to the Greens.

In 1788, Aborigines were dispossessed of their sole residency in this vast and bountiful continent. And that was traumatic for them. And although it sounds callous, that was the way of the world back then. But history cannot be turned back. In international law there is a doctrine called prescription which recognizes that possession of a territory over long period by a new sovereign power confers legitimacy on that power. Edmund Burke said:

> through long usage [prescription] mellows into legality governments that were violent in their commencement.

No doubt, Aboriginal activists would say that Burke means nothing to them (despite that they all enjoy the advantages of our modern society which owes much to Burkean tradition), but the fact is that according to international law, the Commonwealth of Australia is the sovereign power in the continent of Australia and there is no moral (or indeed practical) imperative upon us to cede any part of that sovereignty. There is a moral imperative that we should do all in our power to protect and advance Aboriginal citizens and to respect and allow them to practice their traditional culture to the extent it conforms to the law of the land. This we already do.

Earlier I attributed Aboriginal disadvantage to culture, not race. My view on this is informed by the work of Pastor Paul Albrecht AM, who grew up in the Hermannsburg mission in Central Australia and spent his entire working life in the service of the Aboriginal people. His views are based on his intimate knowledge of the Arrarnta people. He explains that the reason for the plight of traditional and near-traditional Aboriginal people is that they are not able to enter the Australian economy. The mindset that underpins that economy is incompatible with the kinship-based values that are ingrained into traditional Aboriginal children. Put simply, Albrecht maintains that traditional Aboriginal people do not understand the concept of paid work and kinship obligations trump loyalty to the employer:

> Aboriginal culture, termed 'law' by them, is known by the Arrarnta as tjurrunga and covers every aspect of their lives. Tjurrunga is handed down from the spiritual ancestors and is immutable. It cannot be changed by man and as a result, traditional Aboriginals, despite their reputed spirituality, are never called upon to develop innovative philosophical concepts in order to deal with new things. If something is not covered by tjurrunga, for example paid work, then there is no rigorous, consistent and enforceable response to managing it. The same thing applies to the proposed elected Voice supposedly representing all Aboriginal people. There is no such mechanism in traditional Aboriginal culture and those most in need

of help will not understand or buy into its deliberations. They will find themselves marginalized by the articulate, activist, largely urban class. That effect is likely to be worsened by the Voice, which will be dominated by urban Aboriginals who have largely assimilated into mainstream society, while at the same time glorifying an idealized version of traditional culture, the complexities and problems of which most of them do not understand.

Aboriginal culture, like any culture, has no intrinsic value. It is worthwhile preserving only to the extent that it enhances the lives of its practitioners. Or, to be more precise, when it acts against against their interests it, should be discontinued or modified appropriately.

Outside some benign ceremonial and artistic practices, traditional Aboriginal culture has passed its use by date. The most recognizable expression of Aboriginal culture – dot painting – is a recent invention, prompted by the work of white teacher Geoffrey Bardon, who, in 1971, encouraged his students in Central Australia to put their stories onto canvas rather than sand, as they had traditionally done. Dots were then painted over secret portions of the image to conceal them from those not entitled to see them. Eventually, the sacred images disappeared and the dots took over the entire canvas.

Having said that, I acknowledge that people, particularly old people, like what they know and will not abandon it lightly. Their beliefs should be respected. They cannot and should not be coerced into abandoning a lifestyle they have grown up with. If change is to occur it must come through the younger generations and the key to that, as we have always known, is education. It is not my province to prescribe how educational outcomes can be improved but if the Voice could answer just this one question it might justify its existence.

And further, on the spiritual connection with land, Pastor Albrecht says:

> Much is made of the Aborigines' attachment to their land, and of their need to be on their land for their wellbeing. There can be no doubt of the importance that the more traditional Aborigines still attach to their land. However, much of what is said on this subject gives the impression that the Aborigines' attachment to their land is genetic— something they were born with, something they have even when they are brought up in an Australian urban setting, without any knowledge of their own language, and without any in-depth knowledge of the mythology relating to their land.
>
> The Aborigines' attachment to their land has nothing to do with genetics, but everything to do with learning, and the subsequent internalisation of the knowledge that has been passed on. Aborigines were/are animists, believing that the supernatural beings (also known as totemic ancestors) who were active at the dawn of time are still to be found in the land they shaped and fashioned. They also reside in its flora and fauna, in the natural phenomena such as thunder and lightning, in the sun, moon and stars, and in the humans to whom they gave birth. It is these same supernatural beings residing in the land and in the people of that land that gives the Aborigines their unique attachment to their land and their sense of oneness with the land.

For most Aborigines, their spiritual connection with the land will be nothing stronger than an attachment to the land of their birth, exactly the same as it is for me. A well-remunerated Professor of Indigenous Studies living in Hunters Hill has no stronger claim on this land than do you or I.

To sum up:

The Voice, as proposed, looks cumbersome and expensive. It is highly unlikely that any advice it issues will be optimal. Indeed, its advice on practical problems is almost certain to be encumbered with a great deal of ideological baggage.

Proponents of the Voice say 'if you are going to make laws which affect us, we should have a say in the drafting of those laws'. The range of legislation which affects Aboriginal people is vast. And the vast bulk of it is uncontentious. The legislation that specifically affects Aboriginal people comprises enabling legislation and coercive legislation. Enabling legislation is uncontentious and generally the product of lobbying from Aboriginal organizations in the first place. It therefore requires no special advice, over and above what already exists. Coercive legislation, which arguably restricts or discriminates against Aboriginal people, uniquely affects remote and/or dysfunctional communities. It does require rigorous advice, but this is hardly likely to come from a body comprised of the likes of Marcus Stewart, Co-Chair of the Victorian First Peoples Assembly. What unique insight would he, or his 'mob', have into the problems in Alice Springs, for example? And the amount of coercive legislation is dwarfed by the enabling legislation. I have conducted a rudimentary search of all legislation enacted in relation to Aboriginal people by the Commonwealth Parliament since the 1967 referendum. Using the search terms 'Aboriginal' or 'Native Title', I identified 65 separate Acts. Of these only five could be considered coercive, and they all relate to the Northern Territory intervention of 2007. The remainder include those relating to native title (10), land rights (8), land grants (4), education supplementary assistance (5), ATSIC (12), heritage protection (4), land councils (3) and various laws relating to Aboriginal enterprises. I imagine none of these initiatives arose without significant Aboriginal input in the first place. As far as I am aware, none of these laws has ever been challenged as being discriminatory or disadvantageous to Aboriginal people. As a source of advice to government on Aboriginal legislation, this Voice looks like a piledriver to crack a nut.

If the Voice were merely legislated, it would be simple to remove when its work had been done, i.e., when Aboriginal disadvantage had been eliminated, at least to the extent it exists in all other sectors of society. Or if it demonstrated its ineffectiveness.

If a legislated Voice were functioning effectively, it would be a foolish government that terminated it before its time. It would not only be hampering its own efforts but would be exposing itself to electoral retribution.

If the Voice is a practical (as opposed to ideological) imperative, it could be legislated very quickly and at considerably less cost than running a referendum.

Putting the Voice in the Constitution would entrench it there, as a political entity, for all time. It will become a *de facto* Aboriginal parliament.

As part of the Aboriginal sovereignty agenda – which the Uluru Statement tells us it undoubtedly is – it will be the first step in dividing us into two classes of citizens. Those of us whose ancestors (however remote) were here before 1788 and the rest us. And the vast majority of these special Australians are far from disadvantaged – and will become even less so over time. On balance, they are at least as well off as you or I.

Whatever the merits of the Voice, it has no place in our Constitution.

This is not a matter of assuaging, or assuming, the guilt for a process that commenced in 1788. That price was paid by generations of Aboriginal people who had no power to prevent the intrusion of the modern world into a culture that had, hitherto, not advanced significantly in 60,000 years. That process was always going to be painful. There was always going to be a cultural upheaval. It ill behoves current generations of Aboriginal people, most of whom have benefited immeasurably as a result of that process, to try to turn back the clock.

Think very carefully before you agree to corrupt the Constitution, or punish it for the failures of Australian governments – or Aboriginal communities themselves, for that matter – to completely eradicate

Aboriginal disadvantage.

Prime Minister Albanese is trivialising this complex proposal when he describes it as 'only good manners', 'a hand outstretched in friendship' and a 'generous invitation on the part of our first nations people'. He is treating you as a simpleton. Albanese is playing with fire here. By treating this as a moral issue – selling it as a simple proposition and just good manners – rather than what it really is if it gets up – a significant change to our Constitution and a major concession to Aborigines – he is failing in his duty to manage expectations. He has said 'a defeated referendum would be devastating to Indigenous communities'. They will see a defeat as a rejection of Aboriginal people. As nothing more than racism. They will also be angry, but not at Albanese. If it fails – as it should – and if, as I predicted earlier, violence breaks out, Albanese will bear much of the responsibility for this. If this referendum succeeds it will not unite us closer than we already are and if it fails, Albanese is making sure that it drives us further apart. It is hard to imagine a more irresponsible way to prosecute such a major change to our Constitution.

This Voice will not be an end to Aboriginal demands but the beginning of a whole new slew of them. It has nothing to do with reconciliation. If I have not convinced you that the Voice itself is almost certain to be ineffective, I hope I have at least caused you to think twice before agreeing to entrench it in our Constitution, where it will remain for all time. A source of endless, divisive and monstrously costly litigation.

Our society is built upon the Western tradition of the rule of law. A fundamental element of this concept is equality before the law. Putting the Voice in the Constitution, particularly if it leads to some form of Aboriginal sovereignty, undermines this precious doctrine.

Finally, let me re-iterate a point I made right at the beginning. Who we are as a nation – our values and aspirations – is not a function of our Constitution. It is reflected in the democratic traditions and institutions we inherited from Great Britain. And, more importantly, in our legislation, which has made us one of the most diverse, tolerant and generous nations on Earth. It is in our legislation that we must look to enrich all the people, to alleviate disadvantage, to unite us and to recognize past injustices.

Milton Keynes UK
Ingram Content Group UK Ltd.
UKHW011308110923
428462UK00023B/799